Digital Decisions: Choosing the Right Technology Tools for Early Childhood

By Fran Sokol Simon, MEd, and
Karen Nemeth, EdM
Foreword by Chip Donohue

Praise for *Digital Decisions*

Digital Decisions opens up new ways of thinking about technology and young children by offering sound and concrete advice rooted in the everyday realities of early childhood classrooms. It is refreshing to see examples of technology use with young children that feature open-ended play and exploration. Don't miss the book's creative ideas for Skyping with faraway family members to promote cross-cultural discussions, for harnessing the power of mobile voice apps to foster language development, and for employing simple graphing software to help children understand math concepts.

Lisa Guernsey
Director, Early Education Initiative
New America Foundation

Simon and Nemeth have come out with a timely resource on technology that is a must-have for today's early childhood teachers and administrators. Coinciding with the release of the joint position statement on technology in early childhood programs by the National Association for the Education of Young Children and the Fred Rogers Center for Early Learning and Children's Media at Saint Vincent College, this no-nonsense, jargon-free guide helps teachers wade through the wide inventory of technology in all of its forms and select those platforms and devices that will best support the curriculum in developmentally appropriate ways. The authors provide an array of interactive activities that show teachers how to maximize technology as a true learning tool. In addition, each chapter provides supporting guidance for administrators and for those working with children who are dual language learners or who may have special needs. *Digital Decisions* is brimming with charts, resources, and clear judgments that will make a subject that is overwhelming to many easy for all to understand and apply. This is a reference every early childhood program will want to have.

Laura J. Colker, EdD
President, L.J. Colker & Associates
Contributing Editor, Teaching Young Children, NAEYC

For a long time, I have been longing for a book for early childhood educators on digital technology. Now, here's the book I have been waiting for—a treasure trove of practical information, soundly based on the best child development and educational research for young children. Simon and Nemeth anticipate and address your every question with how-to information. Most important, they transform the debate from defining technology as good or bad; rather, showing us how to use technology actively and interactively within good active and interactive early childhood programs.

Ellen Galinsky, President
Families and Work Institute
Author, Mind in the Making: The Seven Essential Life Skills Every Child Needs

Fran and Karen have compiled a treasure trove of great advice and practical suggestions for integrating technology into an engaging and developmentally appropriate early childhood curriculum. From video cameras and iPads to interactive whiteboards and Smartpens, they share the pros and cons of different devices and applications. Even if you are already tech savvy, Digital Decisions will open your eyes and expand your awareness of how technology fits into a purposefully planned, child-centered classroom.

Paula Jorde Bloom, Michael W. Louis Endowed Chair
McCormick Center for Early Childhood Leadership

Digital
DECISIONS

Fran Simon and Karen Nemeth
Foreword by Chip Donohue

Choosing the Right

Technology Tools

for Early

Childhood

Education

Gryphon House
Lewisville, NC

Dedications

To my husband, Mike, who always encourages and nurtures me as I follow
my dreams. Thank you. –F. S.

To my co-author and friend, Karen: Thank you for making the process fun, educational,
and possible. I never could have written this book without your insight, wisdom, and
encouragement. –F. S.

To Marc for teaching me so much about how technology works, and to Vivi and Wyatt for
teaching me so much about how children work technology. –K. N.

To my co-author and friend, Fran: Thank you for sharing your vision, your talent, and your ability
to play nicely in the sandbox. –K. N.

We would like to thank Susan Haugland for her input and for allowing us to build on the
foundation she laid for evaluating early childhood technology tools.

We would also like to thank Chip Donohue for his ongoing support, encouragement, and
mentoring, and for sharing his wisdom with us and with others in our field. Chip's quiet and
steadfast leadership in our community is profoundly impactful.

We are grateful to Larissa Nemeth, Leah Mullen, and Matthew Mullen for their helpful research
and suggestions.

Special thanks to Kathy Charner of Gryphon House for envisioning this project and for nurturing
it and us.

Published by Gryphon House, Inc.
PO Box 10, Lewisville, NC 27023
800.638.0928; 877.638.7576 (fax)

Visit us on the web at www.gryphonhouse.com.

Library of Congress Cataloging-in-Publication Data

Simon, Fran.
  Digital decisions : choosing the right technology tools for early childhood / by Fran Sokol
Simon and Karen Nemeth ; foreword by Chip Donohue.
    p. cm.
  ISBN 978-0-87659-408-7
  1. Early childhood education--Computer-assisted instruction. 2. Computers and children. 3.
Educational technology. I. Nemeth, Karen N. II. Title.
  LB1139.35.C64S56 2012
  372.21--dc23

                        2012000200

Bulk Purchase

Gryphon House books are available for special premiums and sales promotions as well as for fund-raising use. Special editions or book excerpts also can be created to specifications. For details, contact the Director of Marketing at Gryphon House.

Disclaimer

Gryphon House, Inc., cannot be held responsible for damage, mishap, or injury incurred during the use of or because of activities in this book. Appropriate and reasonable caution and adult supervision of children involved in activities, and corresponding to the age and capability of each child involved, is recommended at all times. Do not leave children unattended at any time. Observe safety and caution at all times.

Table of Contents

Foreword

Just in Time

In my work in distance learning, the phrase "just in time" describes the intentional and effective use of technology and distance-learning methods to get the right information to the right person at the right time. As I read this book, I was struck by how the commonsense approach and practical ideas Fran and Karen provide have arrived at just the right time for early childhood educators and administrators.

The 2012 release of the NAEYC/Fred Rogers Center joint position statement, on *Technology and Interactive Media as Tools in Early Childhood Programs Serving Children from Birth through Age 8*, creates a moment in time for early educators by placing the issue of intentional, appropriate, effective, and engaging use of technology and media directly in the spotlight. The position statement raises expectations for educators to be digitally literate technology-mediators, and highlights the need for more and better technology and media training for the adults who work with young children. Fran and Karen have provided a clear pathway to developing technology leadership and improving digital literacy for educators and strategies for effectively implementing the principles and guidelines for the selection, use, integration, and evaluation of technology in early childhood programs.

Our Narrow Bandwidth of Experience

Many of us were "born analog" but live and work in a world where babies are being "born digital" and young children, school-agers, and teenagers are much more digitally literate than we are. Understanding and keeping up with the latest technology tools and interactive media can feel overwhelming and out of reach to those of us who grew up pre-PC and were brought kicking and screaming into the computer age. Yet the technology gap between generations is closing rapidly with the use of smartphones, multi-touch tablets, and other handheld mobile devices as an essential part of our daily lives.

Many early childhood educators feel confident and competent using the latest mobile digital devices to search the Internet, check email, monitor breaking news, get directions, buy tickets, make a reservation, check the weather, take a photo, upload a video, listen to music, update a status on Facebook, post a tweet on Twitter, and maybe even make a phone call. If we can do all of that with our phones, it shouldn't be hard to imagine how technology tools and interactive media can be part of a high-quality, developmentally appropriate environment and learning experience for young children. As our bandwidth of knowledge and experience broadens, the gap between personal and professional use of technology narrows.

A Gentle but Insistent Nudge into the Digital Age

The authors gently nudge early childhood educators and administrators toward the realization that integrating technology will take an intentional and commonsense approach. They offer vignettes that acknowledge the fears and frustrations of educators who feel overwhelmed alongside the effective practices, exhilaration, and excitement of those who have been successful. They invite you to explore, engage, and create with technology—just as you do with any other new open-ended material you're considering for the classroom.

I'm struck by how the goals we have for any appropriate material, such as finding balance; being open-ended; and encouraging meaningful exploration, creativity, problem solving and divergent thinking for the whole child, also define how early childhood educators need to think about how, why, and when to use technology and how best to support healthy media habits for young children. Digital-age educators need to be technology learners, teachers, and leaders. An intentional approach means being open-minded, willing to try new things, able to adjust to changing expectations, and open to teachable moments when the child is the best technology teacher.

Now Is the Time

What an amazing world we live in and young children are growing up in! The Internet, wireless and mobile technologies, and multi-touch devices make it possible to learn with anyone, anytime, in any place, at your own pace, and on a variety of devices. Now is the time to become more digitally literate. Now is the time to gain the knowledge, skills, and experience needed to select, use, integrate, and evaluate appropriate technology tools and interactive media for young children. Now is the time to play with technology tools and try out activities to discover what is appropriate for the children in your care. You're holding the right resource for teachers and administrators. And you've opened it Just in Time!

Chip Donohue
Director of Distance Learning, Erikson Institute
Senior Fellow, Fred Rogers Center for Early Learning and Children's Media

Introduction

Buzzing, Beeping, Flashing, and Blinking: A Dream—or a Nightmare—of a Technology-Driven Day

The alarm on your mobile phone buzzed, but you hit snooze. Now you are late. You jump into the shower and turn on the radio to hear today's weather forecast and the traffic report. It's going to be a hot day for the field trip to the zoo. There is an accident on the main road to work, so you will need to figure out a new route. You grab a cup of coffee from the coffeemaker you programmed last night, and pop a frozen breakfast sandwich into the microwave while you check your email on your laptop. You read the email reminder to bring the classroom iPad, which contains the children's emergency contacts and medical information. You jump into the car and type the address of the center into your GPS to find a new route to work. You dash off a text to the director to let him know you are running late, before pushing the electronic ignition on your hybrid car.

Your day has only just begun, and you have already used a lot of technology to manage your morning and get to work. Does this scenario seems like a normal morning for you, or was this a bad dream of a technology circus run amok? Whether this sounds just like your typical morning or your very worst nightmare, technology is here, and it's here to stay.

What does all of this mean for you as a preschool or kindergarten teacher and for the children you teach? How can you evaluate the tools and opportunities technology has to offer and integrate them into your early childhood classroom so you can offer real-life, hands-on, divergent activities to children? This book will provide you with information, ideas, and resources to help you make your own technology plan based on your experiences and beliefs, the needs of the children, the context of your curriculum, and the resources available to you. Whether you are a technology enthusiast looking for new ideas and guidance about developmentally appropriate practices, whether you are new to the idea of using technology with young children, or whether you are a skeptic, this book is for you.

As you explore how to use technology in your classroom, you may feel overwhelmed at times, but you may also find some digital tools easy to use and incorporate. It will help to realize that you can take just one step at a time. Of course, it also will help to have the support of your supervisor and other colleagues. This book offers guidance and strategies for directors and principals so they can make good decisions about the resources and professional development you will need to succeed. The book will help you and your administrators develop a plan and then explain to the parents in your program the link between developmentally appropriate practice and technology integration in the early childhood classroom. Most of all, this book will offer you the information you need to evaluate the use of technology in your classroom and then apply what you have learned to decide how, why, and what technology is most appropriate and effective for the children in your class.

To Tech or Not to Tech: Finding Balance in the Debate

Because you are reading this book, you are probably looking for information and concrete advice and ideas about how to balance the use of technology-driven teaching tools with more traditional materials and approaches. But, before we get into the details about how to help you make decisions about technology use in your classroom, let's zoom in on some of the concerns many early childhood teachers and administrators have about technology. Rolling back the clock to look at the history of early childhood technology provides helpful insight about how concerns about technology use in preschool settings became one of the most hotly debated issues in our field.

The Early Days of Technology Integration in Early Childhood Education

Since the 1970s when personal computers first became readily available, the idea of using technology—or not using technology—in preschool settings has sparked heated debate in the field. Many early childhood educators saw the enormous promise that personal computers offered. But others were concerned that computers did not fit into developmentally appropriate classrooms. They worried that computers were too complex and abstract for young children. Additionally, because of some practical technology limitations back in those early years of computer usage, educators struggled to determine how to use computers while still maintaining active, lively, and interactive classrooms. In those days, *technology* meant large computers that had to be plugged into power sources and peripheral devices, making them hard to integrate into interest areas in the typical preschool classroom. Their size and need to be "tethered" to power and connectivity limited their applicability in early childhood settings. Also, most of the commercially available software that was available at that time focused on drill and practice, rote memorization, and basic-skill development, not creative, hands-on activities that early childhood educators plan for children. Very few software applications had been developed to encourage divergent thinking and higher-order thinking.

During this period, early childhood educators, universities, and developers began to experiment with technology in the classroom, and a number of computer-based applications were developed for young children. The most significant of these developments began in the 1970s with Logo, a computer-programming language preschool children could actually use to write programs that would manipulate a small robot—called the Turtle—and would create simple graphics. Logo, developed by Seymour Papert, a world-renowned constructivist, student of Jean Piaget, professor at MIT, and the author of *Mindstorms: Children, Computers, and Powerful Ideas*, was revolutionary. The language proved that computers could be used by preschool children in classrooms to encourage divergent and creative thinking and meaningful exploration. This was an exciting development! Over the years, Logo thrived in the background and became the foundation of LEGO's robotics products, but soon got lost amid a sea of commercially developed preschool software. Unfortunately, the more readily available software was, for the most part, not as open-ended and meaningful as the promise offered by Logo. A few good products were adopted by preschool teachers and parents, but it was hard to sort out the good programs from those that were less developmentally appropriate. Toy companies eagerly cashed in on the new availability of computers but with very little understanding of or interest in how young children learn or what represents best practice in early childhood education.

During the 1980s the availability of personal computers and software spawned a proliferation of practice that was less than optimal. Computers were placed in computer labs and children used them during "computer time" (for the most part) to play games that reinforced discrete skill development. Computer time was used as an incentive, and teachers used timers to manage the amount of time children spent in the computer center. At that time, colleges and universities offered courses on technology implementation, but because they were not always required, many early childhood educators graduated with little or even no training in best practice in technology implementation. The early childhood workforce was (and still is) composed of teachers with varying levels of training and/or access to technology, making it difficult to for them to evaluate and integrate technology into their classrooms. The *digital divide*, a term used to describe the lack of access to technology due to cost, training, and opportunity, was profound, and it added fuel to the early childhood classroom technology debate.

There were a few notable exceptions of good software and practice, but overall, the 1980s were hardly a time in which children and teachers experienced the best in developmentally appropriate technology integration. Unfortunately, many early childhood educators formed negative impressions about technology during the 1980s. Since that time, technology tools, integration practices, and appropriate software applications have proliferated and improved, but the stigmas have persisted.

Technology Integration in Early Childhood Classrooms Today

Let's fast-forward to what technology means today: We are no longer forced to use large and extraordinarily expensive computers with wires that bind us to a specific location. We can use our tools almost anywhere, anytime. We are connected to others without boundaries through the Internet. Long-life batteries, small devices, wireless connections, and engaging interactive software applications make it possible to infuse meaningful technology into the nooks and crannies that make up great early childhood classrooms. While there are now many more software applications that encourage creative thinking and imaginative play, it's still difficult to find great software applications in the vast sea of options offered by every conceivable company and developer. The good news is that advances in technology make the sky the limit when it comes to developing tools to do just about anything and everything. Today, true technology integration means much more than using computers and software designed specifically for children to use at specified times of day in specialized areas—it means using still and video cameras, multi-touch mobile devices, interactive websites, graphics and office applications, and many other devices, anytime, anywhere. Throughout this book, you will learn techniques for using many types of applications and devices just as you would crayons, blocks, and prop boxes to achieve the same goals and objectives—to engage children's interests and abilities so they learn and develop in ways that make sense for individual children and for children at various developmental stages.

Since the 1980s a number of important organizations have advanced our thinking and classroom integration practices, providing us with a lot more concrete guidance about how to use technology in early childhood classrooms, including:

- The National Association for the Education of Young Children (NAEYC) Technology and Young Children Interest Forum
- The Fred Rogers Center for Early Learning and Children's Media
- The Joan Ganz Cooney Center at Sesame Workshop
- MIT's Sandbox Summit
- The International Society for Technology in Education (ISTE)
- The Center for Media Literacy
- Ready To Learn, The Corporation for Public Broadcasting
- U.S. Department of Education, Office of Educational Technology

Many of the ideas, tips, and techniques suggested in this book are based on the concepts promoted through these organizations and through practical experiences in preschool settings.

What Does Best Practice in Technology-Rich Programs Look Like?

One challenge early childhood professionals face right now is that many have never seen an example of a twenty-first-century classroom that makes the most of technology by truly integrating and infusing mobile technology tools throughout the classroom and throughout the day. This book will provide descriptions that we hope will bring examples of best practice to life.

As you will see throughout this book, transforming technology in early childhood means the option of using a variety of technology tools from an ever-expanding array of choices in your toolkit. Every day in your classroom, you use crayons, blocks, manipulatives, and other materials to help children learn. Now, you will learn how to evaluate and decide whether to use technology (or not) alongside traditional materials. Technology tools should not be considered replacements for the materials and activities you implement every day; they can simply expand the array of choices you have. Technology tools no longer must be relegated just to the computer area. They can be part of every learning center and interest area in your classroom—as they are in children's homes—making them easier to integrate and use alongside all of the other materials in your classroom. If you decide to enrich your classroom with technology, the most important thing to remember is that adding one digital tool at a time is probably the best route to take. Because advances in digital tools happen every day, adding technology to your classroom should be seen as an evolution. As they say, it's a journey, not a destination.

The Big Debate

So what is the debate all about? While there was certainly discussion about technology use in the 1970s and 1980s, the 1996 publication of NAEYC's first position statement on technology, *Technology and Young Children—Ages 3 through 8,* shined a high-profile spotlight on the use of technology in early childhood programs. Debate about this position statement has lingered over the years, raising more questions than answers about appropriate practice. In addition, since 1996, what is considered to be "technology" has grown to encompass devices and applications we hardly could have envisioned at the time.

In 2009, NAEYC joined forces with the Fred Rogers Center for Early Learning and Children's Media to revise the 1996 version of the technology position statement. The revision, *Technology and Interactive Media as Tools in Early Childhood Programs Serving Children from Birth through Age 8,* was published in 2012, after an unprecedented effort to incorporate all of the legitimate concerns and issues about technology voiced by early childhood educators. Over the two-and- a-half year period in which the new position statement was developed, multiple drafts were published and comments were invited. Several open forums were held to air concerns about technology, and literally thousands of comments were read and sorted to provide guidance on how early childhood educators can effectively and intentionally weave technology into their developmentally appropriate programs.

The ongoing debate about technology centers on a few core concerns:
- *The amount of time children spend engaging with technology in the classroom and at home will dominate their activities and cause them to become obsessed with technology.*
- *Technology tools will be forced into the hands of infants and toddlers.*

- *Children will not be protected from video violence, inappropriate content, and inappropriate marketing tactics.*
- *Classroom technology use will do the following:*
  - *Infringe on or replace play and hands-on activities,*
  - *Stunt imagination and divergent thinking,*
  - *Negatively impact social-emotional growth, and,*
  - *Reduce physical activity and, thus, contribute to obesity.*

These concerns are serious and worthy of careful consideration. Identifying the concerns and fears is important so they can be addressed and so early childhood professionals can use this information to do what they have always done—make decisions about what is best for the children in their programs. This book will offer recommendations, ideas, and strategies that will address the points of contention and will help educators evaluate and then decide how to use technology tools appropriately and meaningfully with children.

Let's take a look at one part of technology implementation that causes a lot of concern: inappropriate practice. Even technology advocates have lingering worries about two issues: software that is overly didactic and/or inappropriate for young learners, and teachers who do not apply principles of developmentally appropriate practice to their implementation of technology experiences. These are very legitimate concerns, and ones that should be considered at the heart of decisions you make. Here's an example:

Suzanne's Concern: Technology Is Developmentally Inappropriate for Young Children

Suzanne, an early childhood educator, observed a kindergarten classroom that uses interactive whiteboards (IWBs) and computers. Suzanne writes, "The children had to sit on the 'listening rug' for 45 minutes of daily interactive whiteboard literacy instruction. Most of the activities were very much like worksheets. For example, in one activity, the teacher called individual children up to the screen to match letters with pictures. At first it was fun for the children, but after a while it became stale. Some of the children squirmed, fidgeted, and ended up in time-out. Overall, the children were uninspired and appeared to be unhappy. They had no recess, no play time, no creative outlets. There were blocks and dress-up areas, but they'd been abandoned for electronic whiteboard worksheet after worksheet and computer lab time."

Suzanne, who is opposed to using digital technology in the early childhood classroom, uses this example to explain why she believes this technology is not developmentally appropriate. We agree that the scenario witnessed by Suzanne is sad, frustrating, and unacceptable. However, the problem was not necessarily the use of the interactive whiteboard technology; the problem was that the teacher's use of interactive whiteboards was just a replication of traditional didactic and boring practices, using technology as the medium. The teacher's practices were not developmentally appropriate. It's possible that if she had not had an interactive whiteboard or computers, the children would have been offered an equally boring and developmentally inappropriate "activity." In this book, we will offer information and practical suggestions about how make the most of digital technology in a developmentally appropriate classroom.

We believe the success of technology implementation in your developmentally appropriate classroom is in your hands. It's about the choices you make: your curriculum, your practice, and how you use *whatever* materials you plan for children to explore and learn from—not whether or not the material is digital. Rejecting technology for your program because it *can be* used inappropriately or because *some* applications are inappropriate is like throwing out the baby with the bathwater! Every teacher and every administrator who intends to use technology needs training, support, and resources as well as time to slowly adapt to the changes, to be successful. With the appropriate training and support, technology tools can and should be a part of your classroom toolkit right alongside the playdough, blocks, and prop boxes.

The Elephants in the Room: Fear, Disruption, and Resistance to Change

Whether it is a new curriculum, new policies, or the introduction of technology, change is often disruptive for everyone who works in early childhood programs. As a matter of fact, change is hard for almost any organization. The fear and resistance that change often incites can be challenging for teachers and administrators alike. That is okay! With challenges come new insights, skills, and understanding. Embrace the process and all of the strong feelings, and then face them! After all, we're early childhood educators, so challenges are not new to us!

> *Jasmine, the head teacher in a classroom for three-year-olds, is a fantastic teacher. She is enthusiastic, creative, and very intentional in her teaching practices. Her classroom is rich with materials that engage children in creative play. She has warm and meaningful relationships with the children and their parents, and she individualizes her practices to meet the needs of every child and every family. In short, Jasmine is a model teacher.*
>
> *When the center received a technology grant to integrate iPads into the classrooms to enhance language acquisition and mathematical reasoning, Jasmine was suddenly lost and upset. For the first time in her seven-year career, she was unsure about how to achieve the goals of a grant. Jasmine was concerned that technology would be inappropriate for her child-centered, play-based classroom. She feared these new expectations would take valuable time away from the routines she had so carefully crafted for her classroom. Visibly upset, she ardently discussed her concerns with the other teachers and in the grant-implementation meeting, where the teachers were tasked with developing technology plans for their classrooms. Marta, the director of the center, was surprised to see Jasmine so worried and confused. She knew implementing the grant would mean a lot of disruption for the staff, but she was unprepared for the emotions this change would bring for even experienced staff members. Marta realized that the cohesive teams she had built might be resistant to change. She readied herself for the challenge.*

Does Jasmine sound like you? Or are you more comfortable with technology? Whether you are technologically savvy or just starting out, it's hard to try new techniques, integrate unfamiliar practices, and adjust to changing expectations. It's easy to rely on established practices. Adding any new practice means spending more time on tasks that were once easy and uncomplicated. It means making time for more professional development and revisiting well-established practices. Initially, change slows things down to what seems like a crawl. It's common to resist change, especially when it comes in the form of technology integration.

No matter how you feel about technology, it's normal to experience some disruption with the introduction of any significant change. If you are resistant, it is important to relax and breathe. Open your mind. Consider all of the options, and try to collect as much practical information as possible. Take it one step at a time. Most important, look for inspiration, guidance, and support from your peers and your supervisors.

If you are among those who are more comfortable and knowledgeable about technology, step up to the plate to support your colleagues. Offer advice, support, and resources. It's time for you to take the lead! You may even find that you can provide your supervisor with ideas and resources that will help everyone succeed.

Interactive Technology versus Passive Media

Much of the debate regarding technology integration in early childhood classrooms has centered on screen time and very broad discussions about technology. The discussions lump all technology into one pot, as if all types offer the same benefits and the same problems. In actuality, there are many kinds of technology—from basic low-tech tools like CD players to complex computers. It is important to remember that some technologies are for passive use, while others support active and interactive use. Lumping everything together in one category doesn't make sense.

Some early childhood professionals believe that all screen time is bad for young children. We hope to show you in this book that all screens are not equal and that all types of early childhood technology should not be lumped into the general term of screen time. The focus of this book is on learning about interactive versus passive technology. Let's take a look at what we mean:

Mr. Cohen's class of four-year-old children sits quietly as they watch a video about healthy snacks. The video lasts about 20 minutes, and several children begin to fidget during the last five minutes. They lose interest and begin to roll around the carpet. The video concludes and Mr. Cohen starts a quick movement activity to get the children's attention and asks them to settle down again. He starts asking questions about the video.

Let's see how much more interactive the experience could have been. Contrast Mr. Cohen's activity with the one offered by Ms. Gonzales:

Ms. Gonzales and the four-year-old children in her class gather around one of the classroom computers as they explore healthy food choices on the USDA's MyPlate site at (www.choosemyplate.gov/). They take turns clicking on various options on the site and talk about the healthy choices and great snacks they see. Ms. Gonzales has created an online voting chart with images of snacks, and the children take turns clicking on the images of their favorite snacks. They chatter about how tall the columns are growing and which column has more votes. One of the options is a class favorite, and one is a new food that some have not tried, so they ask what it looks like. Right away, Ms. Gonzales clicks to navigate to a search engine and pulls up an image to help the children see what they are choosing and compare it to the more familiar choices. She clicks again to find recipes to use in a cooking activity, and she reads the ingredients to the children. They chatter about the ingredients they like and those they don't, "write" (scribbles and inventive spelling depending on their abilities) their own shopping lists, and plan to prepare the dish later that week.

In these scenarios, you can see the difference between using a video and using a computer in the classroom. Watching the video was a passive activity. The children in Mr. Cohen's class sat through most of the video and were engaged in the discussion afterward, but they clearly needed more activity in the moment to capture their interest in digging deeper. Mr. Cohen had to make a note to follow up with more detail rather than capitalizing on the children's interests on the spot.

Contrast Mr. Cohen's activity with the interactivity in Ms. Gonzales's class. The children in Ms. Gonzales's class were engaged throughout the activity. They clicked and discussed throughout the experience, and Ms. Gonzales was able use the Internet to respond with immediate answers, images, and deeper experiences to keep their interest alive.

One activity was passive and the other was an interactive experience. If we had a choice about which one to keep in our classrooms, we would select Ms. Gonzales's interactive activities. Mr. Cohen's activity was not interactive enough to sustain the children's interest and provide the tools they needed to extend their interests.

These examples show that all screens are not alike. Children learn when things happen. They are interested when events occur in real life and on screens, but transformations on television screens and computer screens are completely different. Television requires no interaction to make things happen; transformations and actions just occur on the screen. On the other hand, computers require interaction. Certainly there is more engagement when children can *make* things happen, even with a click or a keystroke.

Dr. Bruce Perry, an internationally recognized authority on brain development and a senior consultant to the Ministry of Children's Services for Alberta, Canada, explains the difference between children's use of technology and television viewing as follows:

> Children are natural "manipulators" of the world—they learn through controlling the movement and interactions between objects in their world—dolls, blocks, toy cars, their own bodies. With television, they watch and do not control anything. Computers allow interaction. Children can control the pace and activity and make things happen on computers. They can also repeat an activity again and again if they choose.
>
> Kneas, K. M. & B. D. Perry. n.d. "Using Technology in the Early Childhood Classroom" on Scholastic Teachers at http://teacher.scholastic.com/professional/bruceperry/using_technology.htm

Ending the Screen-Time Confusion: The American Academy of Pediatrics Statement

In 2001, The American Academy of Pediatrics (AAP) issued a statement, *Children, Adolescents, and Television,* that included findings about television use in early childhood. Many of those findings indicated that screen time is detrimental for young children. Over the years, educators who opposed the use of technology in preschool classrooms used the AAP statements to support their position that all screen time, including computer use, should be prohibited in early childhood classrooms.

Recently, the AAP updated their position. While the AAP still recommends no television time for children under two, a new carefully worded statement released in October 2011 made it clear that the report was intended to provide guidance about passive television viewing, not interactive technology use. All of the research cited and recommendations focused on passive television use at home, not in formal early childhood programs. The report went on to provide encouragement for active "co-viewing" with adults. Even so, we believe there's no compelling reason to include technology in classrooms for children under two. The important distinction in the new AAP report is that all screen time is not equal for children, especially when it comes to preschool classrooms. It's clear that we do need more research in this area, but to date, there is no compelling research that indicates that developmentally appropriate technology implementation by well-trained teachers in preschool programs is detrimental. In fact, significant research, as summarized by Clements and Sarama (2003b), indicates that it can be beneficial.

Our Focus on Interactive Tools

This book is about teachers interacting with children, children interacting with each other, and teachers and children using all kinds of tools—digital and manipulative—to interact with the world. We will not offer suggestions about television, commercially produced video, or other strictly visual media because there are already many books about children's passive consumption of visual media. We will narrow the focus of this book to the tools that offer the most interactivity. Regardless of technology implementation, developmentally appropriate practice is our *only* priority. Given this goal, television and video are not among our preferred technologies: We want children to *do* things and make things happen, not sit back, watch, and listen. We will show you why we think interactive digital tools offer benefits for cognitive, social, emotional, and, yes, even physical development. Interactive technology tools expand the toolkit from which you can choose in your child-centered, play-oriented, and diverse classroom.

What do we mean by "interactivity" as it applies to technology in early learning settings? By interactivity, we mean that children will use tools that allow them to be actively engaged in making things happen with devices and applications. Just as most teachers in child-centered classrooms offer counting experiences with real objects, we will describe techniques, devices, and other tools that you can use to make learning relevant, meaningful, and most of all, appropriate for the needs and interests for the children in your classroom.

The Big Question: How Much Technology Is Too Much?

2

Because there are so many variables in the average day for children in early childhood programs, it's difficult to offer one specific formula for the amount of time children should spend using technology. There are a lot of opinions about time limits. We recommend a couple of rules of thumb.

Infants through Two-Year-Olds

Based on recommendations by the American Pediatric Association (AAP) and other professional organizations, we suggest that infants and toddlers should not spend any time *passively watching* screens. However, limited laptime "co-viewing" of interactive e-books and apps may be something you can consider. In fact, the most recent statement from the AAP highlights the potential benefits of co-viewing. Activities like scrolling through family photos on a handheld device while in an adult's lap, or sharing and talking about a picture book on an e-reader with an adult might be something to consider for toddlers. Co-viewing in a cozy chair as you talk and interact is very similar to snuggling up to read a book. In this case, instead of a print book or a scrapbook, you would be using the electronic version. Or maybe there's just no need to add digital devices to your toddler classroom. That's a decision that's up to you!

That was easy. It's about to get more complicated.

What about Children Who Are Three or Older?

Here's the big question: If you decide to include digital tools in your classroom, how much time should the children spend using them? In the past, many teachers used kitchen timers to set time limits for young children's use of the classroom computer in the "computer area" of the classroom. Children were programmed to stop their work when they heard the *ping*! In today's technology environment—which includes multiple devices and multiple ways to use them—this strict, minute-guided limit is not realistic. Given the average day in a developmentally appropriate early childhood classroom, such a simple directive seems arbitrary. We think it makes sense to structure our recommendations around the real experiences teachers and children might face throughout the day.

Let's look at a typical day. The average routine in early childhood classrooms includes large blocks of time for child-initiated activities (such as free play or choice time) and smaller blocks of time for teacher-initiated or teacher-directed experiences (such as circle time or small-group time). The limits for each type of interaction should be different.

Based on what we already know about attention spans in the early years, we suggest that for children under five, teacher-directed activities during choice time and small-group time should be limited to 20 minutes at a time. This 20 minutes might include the appropriate use of technology. In this case, when activities are teacher-directed, 20 minutes makes sense. Children in kindergarten can usually sustain interest for slightly longer periods of time, so the duration of teacher-directed activities may be longer, but the use of technology in one teacher-directed activity should not exceed 20 minutes.

Remember the scenario in Chapter 1 with Suzanne, the teacher who observed in a kindergarten classroom in which "the children had to sit on the 'listening rug' for 45 minutes of daily interactive whiteboard literacy instruction"? She reported that "the children were uninspired and appeared to be unhappy." Perhaps the interest in the activity could have been sustained if it were developmentally appropriate and had lasted only 20 minutes.

But what about the amount of time children spend using technology during choice time? We think that's an entirely different issue. We suggest that children should be able to spend as much time as it takes for them to complete tasks or satisfy their curiosity, as long as the use of technology is meaningful and intentional. How can we make such a recommendation? Regardless of their choice of materials (technology or traditional classroom materials), we think children need long periods of time to dig into learning and explore without being interrupted. Let's look at an example:

> *Angelique, José, and Tanisha are working together on a mural. They have a long piece of butcher paper, markers, paint, and crayons. They are chatting as they add drawings, and they are talking about what they will add to the drawing next. There are giggles, and ideas are flowing among the children.*

Under most circumstances, in this scenario the teacher would not interrupt this valuable play with a timer set for 20 minutes, unless it was time to transition to another part of the regular routine. Even then, the children would have ample warning that time was about to expire, and they might have been told they could come back to the activity later or the next day.

Contrast the previous example with the following:

> *Angelique, José, and Tanisha are working together using the SMART™ Table drawing application. They are chatting as they add drawings, and they are talking about what they will add to the drawing next. There are giggles, and ideas are flowing among the children. Suddenly, a timer goes off, and Ms. Becker tells the children they must stop and move to another activity. She reminds them that they cannot use technology for the rest of the day.*

Does this scenario make sense? Should we really limit constructive, meaningful play just because the children selected technology as the medium? We don't think so. We also think you may need to consider that, throughout the day, the cumulative amount of time children spend using various technology tools may be more than an arbitrary time limit.

In an article titled, "Limiting Computer Use for Kids" on About.com, Christy Matte, a technologist with CommonSense Media, offers this sound advice:

> Make sure that the time they [the children] have is reasonable for the activity they are doing. It's frustrating to just get started and then have to turn the computer off, so help [the children] choose an appropriate game or activity based on their time allowance.

The article suggests providing children with clear expectations in advance and helping them plan for their technology consumption. In this article, Matte also recommends providing children with visual and auditory cues to let them know when their time is up.

We think if teachers use arbitrary time limits, they may miss important teachable moments and opportunities to help children develop healthy media habits. Instead, offer children tools to track their activities in the various interest areas and with various media throughout the day, and take a look at that use at the end of the week to determine if the time was balanced. Not only will this help them develop healthy media habits, but it will also offer opportunities for children to develop critical self-regulation skills.

> **Example:** You might create classroom diagrams and accompanying cutout icons or photos of the technology tools and other materials in your classroom, as shown in the chart that follows. Then you can offer the diagrams and icons to the children and ask them to affix one icon on the diagram if they used that technology tool over the course of the day. At the end of the week, review the charts with the children and help the children determine if their play was well balanced. Then ask the children to plan where they might play the following week. You might even send the charts home so the children can talk about their experiences with their families.

Weekly Play Chart

List the days of the week, and leave room for children to affix icons in, under the days.

List the interest areas in your classroom, and add a photo of each area.

	Monday	Tuesday	Wednesday	Thursday	Friday
Art					
Blocks					
Cooking Play					
Dramatic Play					
Library					
Manipulatives					
Math Center					
Outdoors					
Water/ Sand					
Writing Center					

Create a set of icons children can use to represent their use of technology each day, such as the ones that follow. Print them out on a sheet of adhesive labels so children can easily peel and paste them on the chart. Remember, you will need a lot of certain icons and fewer of others.

We are not against time-limit recommendations entirely. In fact, we patterned our ideas based on the recommendation made in *The Early Childhood Environment Rating Scale-Revised* (ECERS-R) that no more than 20 minutes should be spent sitting at a computer to play educational games. Here's what we suggest:

Type of Experience	Approximate Length of Time
Laptime co-viewing One child alone or up to three children in a group with an adult close by, if not directly involved	No more than 10 minutes for infants and toddlers, and up to 20 minutes for older children
Teacher-directed activities (group time, small-group time)	No more than 20 minutes
Child-initiated activities (free play, choice time) using open-ended, creative tools	No limit—as long as interest is sustained and learning is evident
Child-initiated activities (free play, choice time) using commercially available software, apps, or websites that are skill or concept oriented	No more than 20 minutes

Your observation and planning skills will be put to the test as you apply these guidelines. You will need to have the big picture in mind of how much time you are spending in teacher-directed activities for the group and know what all of the children are doing individually.

Of course there will be children who seem to want to do nothing but explore technology tools. And, as always, there will be children who will only want to use blocks or art materials. You will continue to need strategies to engage children in various types of play. That's part of what makes you a great teacher!

Developmentally Appropriate Digital Classrooms Look Like This

3

You may wonder what technology looks like in a purposefully planned, child-centered classroom that has a play-oriented environment. We're going to do our best to help you envision best practice. Perhaps the easiest way to draw a picture of optimal digital integration in early childhood classrooms is to compare and contrast appropriate use. As you read the chart that follows, you will see that we have taken a commonsense approach by weaving traditional, well-established concepts of good early childhood practice into the use of technology. You will notice terms and practical advice that you have read time and time again, only this time, we're talking about technology use. You will essentially apply what you already know about great early childhood classrooms to technology and use it just as you would any other material or tool in your classroom. In fact, when you decide to use technology in your classroom, it should be so well integrated that it will not even stand out among the other experiences you offer every day. It will become a part of the fabric of your classroom culture and practices.

In intentional, well-planned, and developmentally appropriate classrooms, technology experiences are integrated into child-initiated play. The use of technology should not outshine or replace any other experiences or opportunities. As you can see in the chart that follows, it's all about balance. We just can't say it enough: Using computers and other technology devices does not mean the end of creative, child-initiated play. In fact, you can use technology to enhance creative play.

Appropriate Technology Use in Early Childhood Classrooms Looks Like This, Not That

Do This (Ideal Practice)	Not This (Not Optimal)
Be intentional with your technology practices: Incorporate technology into your weekly, monthly, and yearly planning for the group and for individual children.	Put technology devices out without planning for their use.
Infuse technology and digital devices into many interest areas in the classroom and offer them as choices with clear objectives.	Only use technology in the "Computer Center" or computer lab.
Use digital tools as options when they make experiences more meaningful or efficient or add value to learning.	Offer "computer time" only as an "edutainment" option during choice time or small-group time.
Use software and apps that help children meet curriculum learning objectives, meet program and state standards, and lead to deeper learning experiences.	Offer technology experiences as rewards or for entertainment purposes.
Select an array of devices, software, and apps that encourage creative thinking and offer multiple divergent learning paths.	Select software that is only designed to entertain or provide didactic instruction on discrete basic skills or computer skills.
Within developmental abilities, balance teacher-facilitated technology activities with those that are child-initiated and independent.	Only allow children to use technology with a teacher in instructional experiences, and never allow independent exploration.
Within developmental abilities, balance child-initiated independent technology experiences with those that involve small and large groups and collaboration.	Only allow children to explore technology in groups.
Extend the learning children initiate during choice time by offering technology as an option to enhance their experiences.	Don't include technology in choice time as an option to extend children's learning.
Develop systems in your classroom to track children's use of technology to ensure they are spending appropriate amounts of time engaging in a range of choices.	Think of technology experiences as "technology for technology's sake." Put out the devices and let children explore them without capturing vital information.

Develop systems to assess children's learning when they engage with technology. Are they meeting appropriate and expected objectives?	Assume children are learning when they are using the computer.

When Children Are Ready for More Challenges

Do This (Ideal Practice)	Not This (Not Optimal)
Station an adult near the computer for help as needed.	Adults go about their business as children engage on their own.
Offer opportunities for exchange of information and communication among the software, children, and teacher, and/or children and their classmates or other members of the school community.	Depend on communication of information from the software to the child. (Instruction or didactic experiences, instead of exchange of information or ideas.)
Engage children in conversations about what they learn or experience on the computer when they work independently or in small groups without adult facilitation.	Allow children to talk among themselves with no additional input from an adult.

What exactly do you need for a well-equipped, intentional digital classroom? Suggestions for Well-Equipped Digital Centers and Classrooms, a chart on page 178–181 of the Appendix, outlines ideas to help you get started, additional ideas for enhancing a good digital classroom, and also a utopian vision of ideal digital classrooms—labeled as "Getting Started," "Good," and "Advanced." Keep in mind that the options are almost infinite and there are no hard-and-fast rules. These suggestions are just starting points to kick-start your thinking and planning, especially if you are perusing grants or other funding.

If you have decided that you want your classroom to include technology tools but are starting from square one, just take it one step at a time. It's more important that you use the tools you have intentionally and well than it is to have a lot of jazzy equipment.

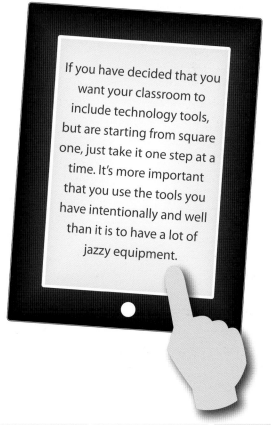

If you have decided that you want your classroom to include technology tools, but are starting from square one, just take it one step at a time. It's more important that you use the tools you have intentionally and well than it is to have a lot of jazzy equipment.

What about Donated Technology?

Free is good, right? Reusing, recycling, and saving money seem like good choices, but there are a few things you should think about before accepting donated equipment. Consider the age and condition of the equipment. If it is too old, it will be difficult to integrate with your overall configuration. For example, if you receive a computer with an older operating system, it may not work with software you want to use or with your printer or cameras. It also may be impossible for you to secure the computers using security and antivirus software. Often, computer donors leave unwanted or inappropriate content on computers, which may appear when children use the equipment. In general, technology manufacturers constantly upgrade and enhance their technology and offer the next new thing. When they roll out a new device or application, it may or may not be "backward compatible," or capable of working with older applications or operating systems. This is a never-ending cycle, so the older the donated equipment, the less likely it is to work with newer products. Over time, you may spend more money upgrading and maintaining equipment than it would have cost to purchase new equipment.

Given the concerns listed above, it still might be a good idea to consider donations, but do so carefully. In addition to considering donations from families, in many communities there are organizations that donate used computers to schools and child care programs. These organizations carefully strip old data and otherwise refurbish the equipment.

Computers— Desktops and Laptops

4

Miss Donohue and the children of her class of four-year-olds gather around one of the classroom computers. Miss Donohue has created a PowerPoint presentation about their upcoming field trip to the local grocery store. She has included photos of the outside and inside of the store, and of the manager who will take them on the tour. Miss Donohue talks with the children about what they want to visit at the store, and she lets them key in their names on the pages that show their favorite parts. As they are talking about the items in their favorite aisles, some questions come up about where things come from. Together, they look up some information on the Internet and select some resources to add to the PowerPoint pages. After the trip, Miss Donohue will add digital photos of the children and their experiences. She'll gather the children around to dictate their memories of the trip so she can type them onto the photo pages. She will email this engaging story of their experience home to the parents, encouraging them to find learning and conversation opportunities in all kinds of everyday activities.

There are computers in many early childhood settings throughout the country. Some are used daily to enhance learning, and some are used as plant stands. The purpose of this chapter is to help you, as an early childhood professional, learn how to make best use of the computer technology available to you in the context of your chosen curriculum.

This chapter will focus on active and interactive aspects of using computers. Although one of the key components of computers is their screens for viewing, computers can be used interactively, not just for passive viewing. As one of the many learning tools in your classroom, a computer adds different dimensions to activities, such as the ability to bring in different languages as needed, or the ability to adjust difficulty levels as children learn new skills. Just as books don't replace music, and music doesn't replace outdoor play, computers do not replace any of the other valuable learning experiences we want young children to have. Computers have the unique role of building early digital literacy skills, such as eye-hand coordination, keyboarding, and responsible Internet use. If you choose to use computers, you can find software to support any aspect of learning you want to cover, and you can find developmentally appropriate ways to use the computer and the software as you go.

There are a number of products on the market for young children that use the name *computer*, though they are smaller machines designed for a particular set of activities. Those will be addressed in Chapter 10. The focus for this chapter will be regular desktop and laptop computers and the equipment that goes with them. One of the first decisions to make is whether you will use an Apple computer (such as an iMac) or a PC (from Dell, Hewlett-Packard, Gateway, or another company). This is simply a matter of preference, availability, and cost. There are advantages and disadvantages for both kinds of systems. For more details to help you make this decision, see the section on Operating Systems in the Appendix.

Operating Systems

Desktop computers and laptops are available from both Apple and from PC manufacturers. The computers have different features and sizes on the outside. Like desktop computers, there are also differences in the way Apple laptops and laptops from PC manufacturers "think"—their operating systems. The operating system of the computer is what creates the user experience. How does the desktop look when you turn on the computer? How are programs listed and accessed? What happens when you save a document? What software can be used? How are things organized and found? How do things move around? While these are important questions, most people can adjust to using either type of operating system.

You can research computers by doing an online comparison search or simply by asking people who have used the versions you are considering. One key factor is that it is easiest if every computer in your program uses the same operating system. When some people have Macs and some have PCs, it is sometimes hard to share information and to help each other solve problems or create lesson plans together. Similarly, it is wise to use computers that are compatible with any other devices in use at your program, such as tablets. When making additional purchases, always check that the equipment or software is compatible with the kind of computer you have chosen. Never assume something will work with both Macs and PCs. The most important thing is to pick one and stick with it so that the different devices and software programs that you have will work together to make your computer experience as easy as possible.

Basic Computer Hardware

The differences between Mac and PC desktop computers are both external and internal. Let's start with the outside. Many PCs have a separate monitor (screen) and central processing unit (CPU). When they are separate, you have to find a place to put the CPU, such as under the desk or on the desk. Adults sometimes place the CPU on a desk and perch the monitor on top of it, but this arrangement may make the screen too high for young children. Look for a safe location in your space to place the computer table or desk. Measure everything. Will the CPU fit under the table or beside it? Is there a nearby electrical outlet and connection to the Internet so wires are close and contained? Make sure the computer will be placed away from the sink or art area, and make sure it does not block areas in a way that might present hazards. Also, avoid placing the computer under a window or in a location where there may be a lot of glare.

One benefit of using a computer with a separate CPU and monitor is that if something happens to the screen, you only have to replace that part rather than getting a whole new computer. On the other hand, the monitor and CPU take up a lot of space. If space is a concern, think about an all-in-one computer like the iMac, with the processing system built into the monitor. Flat-screen monitors for PCs and iMac computers are thinner, so they take up less desk space, but this may also make them more vulnerable to tipping over. If you choose flat-screen monitors, you will need to create a space that protects the unit from being jostled or knocked over.

When planning for your equipment and your space, take into account the different uses for your computer. It needs to be in a location where one or two children can use it undisturbed by noisy activities nearby, and where you can keep an eye on the activity, commenting or helping from time to time. At other times, you may want to be able to gather some or all of the children around as you show them something on the computer, so the placement has to allow for that type of interaction as well.

Monitors come in different screen sizes that greatly influence the cost. In general, larger screen sizes are needed by adults who will use their computers to multitask with several applications open and displayed at the same time. With young children, it will be better to do one thing at a time on the computer, so a smaller screen is probably a better choice. Careful measurements will help you make an appropriate decision for your situation.

Computer Interface

Let a specialist, such as your school-district tech expert, a knowledgeable parent, or a computer salesperson, help you make additional choices, such as what type of mouse to use. Young children seem to be able to use a mouse quite early, but the mouse needs to be very sturdy. Young children—and some adults—transfer the intensity of their efforts to their grip on the mouse. When you are trying to fit that last puzzle piece in, you might instinctively pound the mouse just like you'd pound the puzzle piece! Several early childhood suppliers offer specially designed computers and computer stations in their catalogs. These are not necessary, but they do offer additional design and support advantages that you may want to consider.

Another hardware option is a touch-screen computer that allows children to make things happen with the tips of their fingers on the computer screen. This makes learning how to use the computer easier for younger or less-experienced children, or children with special needs. Still, remember that for many applications, children will need to learn to use a mouse to make things happen on the screen. The younger the child, the better results you will have with a touch screen. Using a mouse is a different skill that requires understanding and coordination.

Wireless keyboards and mice are available that communicate with the computer via Bluetooth technology. These tools are great for adults but may not be sturdy enough to be tossed around by little hands. If funding is available, you might consider getting a wireless keyboard or mouse to use when you want to stand back and show the children something on the computer. These devices free you from having to sit at the desk with children crowding around.

Computer Connectivity

When planning the computer landscape of your classroom or program, think of Internet access as a vital component that adds incredible depth and life to the learning that can happen with computers. Whether you connect to the Internet via an Ethernet cable and modem, or you choose to use a wireless hub, Internet access will elevate the effectiveness of your computer implementation. More details about making these decisions is covered in Chapter 5.

Peripherals

Items attached to computers are called *peripherals*. This additional equipment can add value to the computer experience in your early learning environment, and examples might include cameras, microphones, and printers. As you find more and more opportunities to use computers in developmentally appropriate and creative ways, having a color printer on hand becomes increasingly useful. Children can create signs, gameboards, menus, costumes, storybooks, and records of scientific observations and print them out to add to their play. You can print out examples of what children worked on and send these examples home with parents on the same day. Most new models of desktop and laptop computers have built-in cameras and microphones, but you can buy these if needed. They allow children to record their own messages, stories, or skits, and they make it possible to connect with people all over the world on videochat platforms, which are discussed in Chapter 10.

Laptops

A laptop computer is a fully functional computer that is designed to be used wherever the user is sitting, rather than staying in one place as a desktop does. Laptops are made by many different companies and have many different features. You can choose Apple laptops that use the same operating system as the Apple desktop computers, or you can choose laptops from a variety of manufacturers that use PC operating systems. Most laptops have screens that flip open and closed. Although it is rare to see laptops in early childhood classrooms, children may be familiar with them at home. Laptops can be more expensive than desktop computers and may not be as durable. The flipping-up-and-down action of the hinge leaves it vulnerable to breaking. Battery life may not be sufficient to keep the laptop going all day. However, some laptops are being specially designed to bring computer learning and wireless Internet access to children in remote areas of the world.

One organization is One Laptop per Child (http:// one.laptop.org}. The laptops created for this organization are especially durable and have extraordinary battery life. They are not widely available to the public yet, but elements of their design may find their way into the early education market before long. Yes, laptop computers are more portable, but there are other mobile devices that are easier to carry from place to place as learning is happening. Mobile devices and tablets will be covered in Chapter 7.

Technical Support

If you are not totally comfortable with computers yet, you may wonder what they can contribute to an early childhood classroom. We recommend that you visit some classrooms where computers are used actively by the teachers and the children. It is not necessary for you to become a computer expert. Help is always available (see the list that follows this section). You can add technology to your program one step at a time. Computers are a lot like shoes—they may look pretty, but what's comfortable on someone else might make you miserable. Don't make any major purchase until you've had a chance to try it out. That may mean buying one computer for your program and piloting the machine and the software until you are sure it will work for you before adding more. One thing's for sure: Whatever technology you buy today will be surpassed by something new before long. If you pass up a chance to buy something today, there will always be something—and it might be better—available later, so there's no need to rush into anything.

If you choose a Mac computer (from Apple) or a PC (from Dell, Hewlett-Packard, Gateway, or any other company), or some other version, the manufacturer is likely to have videos or a support system to help you have a positive user experience. That's always a good place to start. In fact, that could be a deciding factor. Many directors base their technology purchasing decisions on what kind of support comes with the purchase. Here are some additional options for finding help with your technology efforts:

- The websites of state departments of education often provide information about selecting and using computers.
- Local school districts generally have one or more technology specialists who should help you if you are part of the district and might help you even if you are not.
- Your local computer store may have someone on staff who is trained to work with educators to help them to select products.
- Public libraries are gaining ground in the field of using technology for learning so they may have people or resources to help you before and after you purchase your computer.

- Some national organizations have a technology special interest group, such as NAEYC's, found at www.techandyoungchildren.org. Other groups, such as the International Society for Technology in Education (www.iste.org) are devoted to the effective use of technology in the classroom.

- You can set up a professional learning network or join one that is already established. State and local chapters of national organizations can be a good place to look for other early childhood professionals in your area who are interested in sharing technology ideas, questions, and resources.

Infusing Basic Technology and Computer Skills into Your Lesson Plans

The first step is for you to help the children use computer hardware successfully to support their learning. Here are the basic hardware skills you will want to support in your work with the children. Some of these may vary depending on the type of computer(s) you are using.

- Turning the computer on, starting and stopping programs or activities
- Understanding the safe use of hardware: no banging, hitting, bumping, knocking; no liquids or moisture; no pulling cords or sticking things in anywhere without permission
- Making the connection between moving the mouse and what happens on screen
- Understanding the cursor—what it is, its different forms and functions, and how to use it
- Clicking the mouse, highlighting text, dragging items
- Drawing with the mouse or by touching the screen
- Keyboarding skills—typing letters, then using punctuation, numbers, and capitalization; using function keys such as delete, return, or space bar
- Undoing, erasing, going forward and backward from one screen to the next
- Using appropriate touch-screen and multi-touch gestures, such as swipe, touch and drag, and double tap
- Understanding icons, how they are used, what they mean
- Understanding and using input devices: disks (CDs or DVDs) and flash drives (also called memory sticks, ThumbDrives, or JumpDrives)

Learning How to Use Computers

Digital literacy, which is described and discussed in depth in Chapter 13, is a key component of computer knowledge and skill. As children learn the skills for operating the machines, they should also be learning how to use those machines responsibly, which includes well-planned practice, helpful activities, and a bit of open-ended exploration. Young children seem almost fearless when they encounter a new technology, and they are often willing to just start trying it out immediately. Keep in mind that young children approach technology without preconceived notions or self-doubt, and they can learn about technology through hands-on exploration just as they learn to explore and understand other materials in the classroom and in their world. Guided practice and a chance to just "mess around" are two learning strategies that seem to work better for young children than didactic lessons. And, of course, having the right technology available is important for this learning.

Media literacy, which is also described and discussed in Chapter 13, is part of digital literacy. With the benefits of access to vast information resources comes a risk for misuse or inappropriate information. It is very important that you consider how to infuse commonsense use, safety, and security into every technology experience in your classroom by making these experiences teachable moments. For example, when forms appear on a website, help the children understand why they should never share their personal information online, unless an adult does it for them. Talk about "stranger dangers" online, and as the children get older, expand the discussion to include the tactics of companies who sell products online.

Developmentally Appropriate Activities for Preschool/Kindergarten

Young children may be able to turn on the computer, select the game or activity they want, and get it started. This means that computer activities may be made available as an option during choice time, work time, or free play when children can choose the computer and do the activity without constant support from an adult. Preschool and kindergarten children also benefit from working together, perhaps with one or two other children at the computer to play, take turns, or collaborate on solving a problem.

Now let's look at some ideas for using computers to meet learning goals in several domains.

Logic and Reasoning: Computers can offer many experiences that support the development of logic and reasoning skills like problem solving. To meet this type of learning objective, it would be best to make the computer available for children to work alone or in pairs to solve problems, establish priorities, or make decisions. Save each child's work so you can track which children use logic and reasoning activities at the computer, and you can check to make sure that everyone has had a chance to accomplish those objectives.

Thinking and Learning: Think of the computer as a tool to support curiosity and creativity throughout the classroom. Wherever children are playing, exploring, or making things, they should know that answers to many questions can be found with an Internet search on the computer. Building a block tower and wondering how to turn it into a bridge? Look up models on the Internet! Wondering what baby dolls wear in China? Look it up! Trying to remember a favorite song from last month? You don't have to wait a few days to get the answer. Also think of the computer as a great recorder—a place to save searches, notes, and pictures that support that all-important project-based learning that extends across days or even weeks.

Math: Mathematical thinking shows up very frequently in early learning software packages, but you don't have to buy software to put your computer to work as a tool for math learning. Wondering which has more players, a baseball team or a basketball team? Look up pictures of your local favorites. Why talk about the numbers of legs on ants, spiders, and centipedes when you can show children pictures and count the legs? Use programs that already come with your computer, such as the calculator, timer, or Excel spreadsheet, to practice and explore math concepts.

Science: Use the computer to record observations of science explorations. You might upload photos taken with a digital camera, use a drawing program that allows children to draw what they see with the mouse or touch screen, or use an Excel spreadsheet to count how many times children observe certain characteristics. Search for information on the Internet about bugs you have observed in the yard. Show brief videos from websites such as www.youtube.com, www.teachertube.com, or http://kids.nationalgeographic.com/kids/ to illustrate biology and physics concepts you want children to understand.

Creative Arts: Download software so children can play and record their own music on the keyboard. Classical artworks can be researched and displayed as models for the art area. You can even work with children to research different ways to make your own playdough.

Language Arts and Literacy: Learning to use the keyboard and finding the letters and characters not only contributes to computer literacy but also to literacy in general. Allow children to use the capabilities of a computer to collect, record, embellish, and play back stories, notes, instructions, and poems.

Social Studies: Explore the home countries of the children in your class, or research different countries and cultures. For example, you might do a study about the similarities and difference of police uniforms and vehicles in different countries. Use the computer to create culturally appropriate displays for the classroom.

Technology for Dual Language Learners (DLLs), Point #1

When planning a classroom that is appropriate and responsive for children who speak different languages, computer hardware should always be on the list of must-haves. Across the United States, language diversity is growing fastest among the population of young children. Approximately 25 percent of children under the age of six come from immigrant families. This means that any early childhood teacher in any part of the country may encounter a classroom with not one or two but more likely three or more languages. Moreover, as you prepare materials and activities in the languages you have this year, you may find that next year you have to start over with new languages.

Use your computer to find and store information, stories, and resources in the languages of the children in your program. You will be able to print out labels for the areas of the classroom and for keywords in storybooks. When volunteers can help you translate words into hard-to-find languages, you can use the words to create activities, books, and displays for the children who need them. This strategy will make it possible for you to make changes at a moment's notice when a new child arrives, and to share what you have developed with colleagues, so they can meet the needs of their diverse students as well.

Assistive Technology for Children with Special Needs, Point #1

Computer hardware is an important component for inclusive early childhood programs. In addition to your computers, monitors, and printers, you may find that specially designed assistive technology add-ons are needed by some children to make sure they have access to the same learning experiences as their classmates—and you need the computer first to enable the use of those specialized devices.

Children with vision differences may benefit from viewing the pages of a storybook on a large, brightly lit computer screen. Children with motor differences may be able to demonstrate their interests and learning by using large, adaptive buttons and switches. Children who have health issues that cause them to spend a lot of days at home could still participate in the activities of your program via a computer. If assistive devices are required by the child's individualized education plan or family service plan, they may be covered by state or school-district funding or by the child's health insurance. We also suggest you contact your local special education resource centers to learn about the hardware that may be available by loan.

Sometimes the most valuable hardware for children with different needs will be the furniture that makes it possible for them to sit comfortably and reach what they need to reach. Look online and work with therapists to buy or create furniture adaptations that provide the best computer experience for children with special needs.

Sample Technology Lesson Plan #1:
ALL ABOARD THE TECHNOLOGY TRAIN!

Purpose
To acquaint the children with the educational technology available in your classroom

Target ages
This flexible activity can be adapted for any age.

Learning objectives
- Approaches to thinking and learning: Children will interact with each piece of technology in the room.
- Health and safety: Children will remember basic rules for safe technology use.

Keywords

button	cord	monitor	screen	volume
click	keyboard	mouse	speaker	
computer	laptop	printer	switch	

Preparation
Before the activity, create a simple map of the classroom with the key hardware items clearly indicated. Create labels with the same hardware images so each child gets a sheet of labels. The items that must not be touched should be colored red. Turn on the hardware and set it to a particular program or game that will be easy to demonstrate.

Materials
conductor's hat and whistle
printed copies of your map and labels

Activity
Give each child a copy of the map. Be or assign a child to be conductor, who will wear the hat and blow the whistle. Line up like a train and follow the map to the computer. Give children a chance to put their labels in the right places on their maps. Demonstrate a quick computer game and give each child a chance to touch the keyboard, mouse, screen, and so on. Talk about why there is a red label for the cord—because it is not safe to touch. Then send a page to the printer, and move the train to the printer. Again, let the children place their labels on the spot on the map for the item they have found.

Save the maps for reminders and additional discussions about what technology is in the room and how it will be used. Bring out a child's map when you have a chance for an individual or small-group conversation with him or her, and use the map to work with the child to find out which types of hardware are already familiar and which seem unfamiliar so you can plan future activities accordingly.

For younger children, just use the train format to visit the technology items in the room and, get a sense from their reactions whether or not they may have encountered that kind of hardware in the past.

411 FOR DIRECTORS AND OTHER ADMINISTRATORS: COMPUTERS—DESKTOPS AND LAPTOPS

Important Considerations

Mac or PC
This debate will rage on forever. Macs may offer a certain amount of protection from malware and viruses and tend to be more user-friendly, to be easier to integrate, to have better support, and to be more reliable.
The tradeoff: Macs offer fewer options for software and have a higher cost. PCs are more affordable and have a huge range of software options.

Laptops or desktops or both
A combination of both is ideal, but if you have to start with one or the other, laptops will provide more flexibility.
The tradeoff: Laptops are less durable and more prone to theft.

The number of computers needed
This is likely to be driven almost completely by your budget, but we've offered some very flexible guidelines in the table in the Appendix on pages 178–181. Certainly, the ideal would be to have at least one computer for children and one for adults in each classroom, but sharing among classrooms is always an option. Computer labs (all computers located in one room) are an option but really don't allow for true integration into the classroom or into the curriculum being implemented in the classroom. Ideally, computers can be spread throughout the center, and if they are shared, they are moved about as needed.

Furniture for stationary machines
Standard child-sized classroom tables and chairs will work, but having a specially designed ergonomic computer station is ideal and may be required to meet the needs of children with special needs.

Professional development

Providing training and ongoing coaching, mentoring, and technical assistance for administrators and teachers are critical components of successful technology integration. You can have every bell and whistle in the technology toolbox, but if no one knows how to use the tools or if staff members use them incorrectly, the tools will be ineffective.

Being successful with developmentally appropriate technology integration depends on your ability to identify technology leaders in your program and engage them as mentors and advisors for the entire staff. While there are often great resources in your local community or online, having internal technology champions for day-to-day coaching is ideal. Because monitoring, assessment, and evaluation will be important to ensure ongoing appropriate technology implementation, you may also need to engage in ongoing professional development to keep your own tech skills sharp.

To jumpstart formal professional development, first check with the companies that sell your equipment and software. They often offer free professional implementation training or reduce the cost in order to get you to sign on the dotted line. You can certainly try to negotiate this into your purchase. You can also check with your local Child Care Resource and Referral Agency and other organizations in your area for hands-on live training if possible. You can also look for online training. But remember, there is no substitute for ongoing, on-the-job coaching and mentoring.

Professional development will be a big budget item in your plan. You may need to make hard choices to balance the desire to purchase a lot of cool technology with the desire to provide the ongoing professional development your staff will need in order to effectively use that cool technology. If there is ever a choice, opt for fewer tools and more support! **The tradeoffs:** The staff, children, and families in your program may experience frustration and failure if they are not supported with the knowledge they need to use the technology tools in your program. Balancing the cost of professional development with the cost of equipment will help you plan the resources you need for everyone to experience some measure of success.

Plan for tech support

Set aside at least 5–20 percent of your overall tech budget for tech support and maintenance. If you are just getting started with new equipment, the cost will be lower, but as the equipment ages, the demand for maintenance and repairs will go up.

Computer Software, Apps, and Activities

5

Mr. Mullen noticed that three children in his four-year-old class needed extra practice in recognizing letters of the alphabet. He opened a letter-recognition game from www.starfall.com on the computer so it would be ready for them when they chose the computer area during free play.

If hardware is the brain of the computer, software is the computer's thoughts and ideas. Your computer comes with some software built in. You might buy additional software on disks or might order software that you download from the Internet (if your classroom computer is hooked up). There are thousands of cloud computing websites that host the software and allow you to use it at no cost or for a fee when you visit the site. When you choose this kind of software or activity, you won't have to hold onto disks or buy new disks for each device that uses that activity. For example, the International Children's Digital Library website (http://en.childrenslibrary.org) allows visitors to view and read children's books from different countries on any computer or mobile device without having to buy, borrow, or store the books in the classroom.

> *If hardware is the brain of the computer, software is the computer's thoughts and ideas.*

Software designed to help you or the children perform a particular set of tasks or activities is called an *application*—also known as an *app*. There are apps for PCs, Macs, and mobile devices of all kinds. Some are designed specifically to support learning goals, and some are just for fun. Some apps are free, some are low cost, and some can be quite costly. In this chapter, we will discuss how to select and use software and applications for desktop and laptop computers.

Appropriate Computer Software, Apps, and Activities

When you are considering the software, activities, apps, and games that could be used on your computer, you will see that the range of quality and appropriateness extends from very low to very high, and there is a confusing array to choose from. Refer to the chart on pages 178–181 for step-by-step guidance about making purchase decisions. Keep in mind that it's not just about the quality of the application itself—it's about how it will be used. Think about the puzzles in preschool classrooms. Is a puzzle a good thing or a bad thing? Well, it depends on how it is used. A puzzle that is too easy or too hard for the children, or that no one ever talks about or uses, may not serve as a high-quality element in a classroom. But a puzzle that provides the right level of challenge and that focuses on a topic that supports a lot of conversation may provide very high-quality engagement.

Choose software, activities, and games that are developmentally appropriate. Look for programs that support interpersonal interactions, interactions with the software or Internet, problem solving, creative expression, engaging language, and multiple levels of play. Just as you strive to ask open-ended questions when talking with children, you want computer software to provide open-ended activities and divergent paths for children to explore.

You may purchase software on CDs or DVDs in online or "big box" stores, but more often than not, downloading software from the Internet for a fee is a more efficient way to purchase and then install software on your computer. Software developers prefer to provide software over the Internet to lower their costs; they also provide easy updates over the Internet.

There are wonderful programs that address early literacy, math, science, language and culture, art and design, fine motor activities, social studies, health and nutrition, and music. If your computer is connected to the Internet, you can find many free or fee-for-service websites that provide similar activities. For example, www.readingrockets.org provides literacy activities for children, teachers, and families. The Public Broadcasting System (PBS) offers online science activities for young children at http://pbskids.org/zoom/activities/sci/.

Using Grown-Up Programs for Early Learning

There are many ways to use the software found on most adults' computers to accomplish early learning goals. In fact, this is an important part of technology learning, as children also need to know how *you* use computers. If you spend the bulk of your computer budget on machines and training, you still may be able to do a lot without purchasing expensive educational software for your children. Let children see you type the weekly parent update in Microsoft Word and print out 20 copies. Show them how you use http://translate.google.com to create versions of the update in the languages you need. Then, you might set up writing activities so the children can dictate or type stories and notes to parents on Word and click Print to make their writing appear on paper.

You can also work with children to show them how to play with different fonts and sizes, or with WordArt (a feature of Microsoft Word that lets you create artistic, curvy lines of text and individual letters) as they work on recognizing different letters. You might let them dictate a story that you type in, then make all the letter *B*s extra-large so the children can practice saying the /b/ sound. You can use Excel to make lists and charts and graphs, and change or add to them over a period of days. Show children how to do an Internet search for pictures. Let the children help you think of keywords on a topic you are interested in looking up together. For example, if the children are interested in playing "restaurant" in dramatic play, will they get more ideas by typing *table* or *dinner* in a search engine? We think of keywords as an artifact of the computer age, but keywords can also be clues to refining your understanding of a concept. To show that you really understand what a restaurant is, you have to know it is not just a building with tables in it, but a place where you sit and order dinner. It's the keyword *dinner* that distinguishes a restaurant from a bank or library, which also have tables.

Getting ready to go outside? Look up the weather on the computer. Want to connect the children in the class with their extended families? Explore what the weather might be like where the children's grandparents live. Have 20 cookies and 15 children in your class? Make a table with 20 squares, and color in 15 of them one by one so you can see if there will be any cookies left over, and discuss what to do with them. Looking for a song that uses new vocabulary words that the children are learning? Use PowerPoint, Keynote, or other presentation software to post the words to a new song (or add the new words to a familiar song) so the children can follow along, and insert pictures to illustrate the movements they should be making as they sing. All of these ideas help children learn what they need to learn, but they can learn those things while using the regular software that we use and that they will use when they get to elementary school.

You may also use some of the basic programs borrowed from adult work, such as Microsoft Excel (described in the Miss Donohue vignette on page 35). You might use Microsoft PowerPoint or Apple Keynote to gather images and information for a changing display of a classroom project. Consider the following example.

> *Miss Deedee took pictures documenting the progress of a building that three children were making in the block area. Then she inserted each photo onto a slide in a PowerPoint presentation. She added captions that were dictated by the children who made the building, and set the slideshow to change automatically on the classroom computer—visible by the other children and by the parents as they came to pick up their children.*

Digital Music Software

A specific example of adult software that has become widely used in early childhood education is the free iTunes program that anyone can download onto their computer from the Internet. iTunes is considered a media player software. With media player software such as iTunes, you can not only purchase and download songs and albums digitally, but you can also load all the music from your CDs onto your computer and organize the music. Now, instead of a box of CDs with fixed songs on each one that you have to look through one by one, you can search for individual songs by keywords and pick from various sources all in one place to meet your needs. You can create playlists for occasions, for languages, for certain word sounds or rhymes, for anything you can think of. And if you need songs to illustrate a certain topic or to support a certain language, you can download an individual song that is just what you need without having to buy the whole album.

Songs are not the only resources available via iTunes. You can keep audiobooks, videos, movies, and TV episodes. You can even convert videos you find online at such sites as www.youtube.com or www.teachertube.com and save them to your iTunes library.

Keep in mind that, once these items are saved, you can play them on your computer, your MP3 player, your mobile multi-touch device, or even your interactive whiteboard because iTunes can share with all of these devices. When devices share, or *sync*, with iTunes on a computer, the information you have selected—which can include songs, photos, audiobooks, apps, and playlists—is copied onto another device. The devices also receive software updates that help keep the devices continue in good working order. You can create targeted playlists and load them onto the classroom's MP3 players so you can control the content and be sure children are using them for learning purposes.

Now, with Internet access, music is so much easier to find. With MP3 players, it is so much easier to use and store. With all of your music at your fingertips, you may find more ways to incorporate it into the day. While we do not recommend having music on in the background all the time (it interferes with speech perception and conversation), you might be surprised at the bits of learning time that can be enhanced with a song or two. Think about singing educational songs while lining up or waiting for a snack. Sing songs to remind everyone of the rules for a field trip or to motivate everyone at clean-up time. Take home a playlist of bilingual songs for yourself to practice and learn different languages. And, by all means, use music to engage and involve families, too. You can even share the classroom iTunes files with parents. They can download the songs to their phones, MP3 players, iPads, and other devices so they can enjoy the music at home, as described in the following scenario.

> *Miss Madhavi searched through her media player library on the computer and created a playlist of songs featuring healthy foods in English and Spanish. She then synched* the classroom MP3 players with the computer. During the day, she played some of the songs during a music activity and during transitions to add a learning element. Children were allowed to bring the preloaded MP3 players home over the weekend so they could practice the songs and extend the learning with their families.*
>
> **Sync means to make the files (in this case, music files) match on both devices—in this case, the music on the computer transferred to the MP3 players.*

Another benefit of using digital music storage is that it does not take up space in your classroom. Wouldn't it be nice to get rid of your boxes and boxes of CDs? Most teachers don't allow young children to dig through their collection to find music they want to play. With digital music players, however, children can search independently through playlists and can find music that interests them. You will need to listen to every song and have colleagues or parents help you review songs in other languages to be sure they are appropriate, before making music available to children. Don't forget to keep your personal music library separate from the children's library, just to be sure there's no confusion. You will also need to establish policies and practices to avoid copyright infringement. This book is not a legal resource, so we leave it up to you to identify your needs and get advice about how to handle them.

On page 59, you will find The Commonsense Approach to Developmentally Appropriate Evaluation of Software, Websites, and Apps Developed for Young Children, which provides information that will answer many of your questions and concerns about evaluating software and activities for your classroom. The next section provides ideas for developmentally appropriate activities.

Including Software, Apps, and Website Activities in Lesson Plans

The NAEYC technology position statement reminds us that developmentally appropriate use of technology requires careful consideration of each child's age and ability. To meet the learning goals you have for the children in your care, informed and intentional planning will be an important task. Match the activities to clearly defined learning objectives for best results. Rather than saying, "This computer game teaches math," you should be able to describe the specific ways it will help the children in your class. For example, the game you have chosen will help Johnny, Susie, and José learn to identify shapes and will help Joon, Emily, and Hannah learn to make patterns using three or more shapes. It is not necessary to use a simple computer program to duplicate or replace an activity that children can easily do without the computer. Also, avoid simplistic activities that are just a gimmick on the computer. Try to find activities for which the computer adds a dimension to the learning process and encourages active participation in the activity.

Take some time to examine your lesson plans for the coming week. As you look over your plans, think of one or two activities each day that could be enhanced by using a computer. For example, if you often use graphing activities, plan to gather the children at the computer one day as you use Excel to chart their responses to a question about the colors they are wearing. (Create the chart in advance so it is ready to go.) Once you try this and see how the children react, that will help you think of more ways to use this kind of computer software activity and add it elsewhere in your lesson plans. As you become more familiar with the technology planning process, you will learn many more ways to embed computer software and app work and other options into your plan to further your learning goals. You will also learn new ideas to make developmentally appropriate computer software and app activities available as part of free-choice time. Try new activities in small doses—one at a time.

Developmentally Appropriate Activities for Preschool/Kindergarten

Technology-based learning activities have to be more than fun, more than cute, more than enticing. Always keep the principles of developmentally appropriate practice (Bredekamp & Copple, 2010) in mind when making software and app choices. What is appropriate for one child in your group may not be appropriate for another; what is appropriate for one group of children may not be appropriate for another group. Think of ways to individualize experiences and activities. For example, young children may enjoy activities that use computer-generated characters (called *avatars*) that can be modified to represent the child and show the child's name. This will help the children have a more personalized experience with the activity and may give them a sense of power and control over the activity. Here are some ways that software, apps, and website activities can help preschool and kindergarten children meet learning objectives:

Logic and Reasoning: Look for activities that promote true problem-solving skills, by presenting appropriately complex situations and real-world examples, such as games that offer choices between a slower, safer path, and a quicker, riskier path.

Thinking and Learning: While very young or inexperienced children may benefit from immediate feedback as they work on computer activities, children develop the skills they need to be effective learners through curiosity, exploration, and persistence. As the children become more experienced with the computer software, provide activities that require multiple steps before feedback is provided or that allow for a variety of explorations driven by the child's interests. The children's curiosity should be encouraged rather than stifled.

Math: There are many programs that offer basic counting experiences. Look for added features that engage children, provide variety, and have the ability to increase the level of challenge as children progress. Interact with the children as they learn to count the things in their environment, and then support that learning with appropriate computer programs. Software is also available to help children learn and use shapes; to measure and compare things; to group, add, and subtract numbers; and to create patterns. There are also several websites that have online math activities for children to play and practice math skills.

Science: There are many software programs available to provide science activities for young children. However, what they need to develop scientific thinking—observing, describing, recording, watching for change, guessing and testing, comparing results—are all skills that can be practiced using adult software, such as word-processing programs, spreadsheets, or photo-storing programs. For example, children might draw an insect they find on a piece of paper and then go to the computer to look up several detailed photographs of insects and compare the attributes until they can select the picture of the example they drew.

Scientific knowledge encompasses biology, physics, chemistry, and environmental science. That sounds like a lot for a young child, but the truth is their boundless curiosity about how the world works is perfectly suited for this kind of science exploration. Websites for organizations like NASA, National Geographic, or a regional zoo are just some examples of the kinds of rich, engaging science information that can ignite children's excitement as they learn more about the science concepts that they initially experienced in classroom hands-on activities.

Creative Arts: There are many wonderful programs, such as those for drawing and writing, that allow children to use the computer to create their own artistic pieces. Children can play with different lines, mixing colors, or positive/negative space. In addition, you can find vast collections of real artwork that you can study and discuss as the children create their own drawings. However, remember to use software only to supplement, not replace, hands-on art activities. Think of computer programs as one of the many art-expression tools you provide for children. You might also provide software for recording or playing music.

Language Arts and Literacy: You will want children to practice all four of the components of language and literacy. Look for software or programs that promote speaking (by recording children's poems or conversations), listening, reading, and writing (which could be typing on the keyboard or making letters on the screen with their fingers). Using the Internet, you will also be able to help children learn literacy skills in their home language and in the languages of their friends. A number of websites provide free literacy resources and activities. Sometimes these are offered by companies as a service in hopes that you will also visit their site to make a purchase, but there's no obligation. For example, the Barnes & Noble bookselling website has recordings of celebrities reading children's books that also show the pages of the book. Other organizations, such as Reading Rockets, receive funding to offer literacy games and activities as a service to the community.

Social Studies: It is important for children to learn about the people around them and how people work, play, and live together. You might use software to create a cast of characters for an imaginary city, or you might go online to explore what different people do in their jobs. It is, of course, wonderful when parents or other volunteers visit the classroom to talk about their work. But some year you are going to have a class full of children who are fascinated with pets and want to be veterinarians, but no volunteers in that field have come forward. If this happens, there are videos and photos of veterinarians at work if you search the Internet or YouTube. Technology allows you to keep the non-tech aspects of this exploration while enhancing and filling in gaps with the advantages of technology. Or imagine if a volunteer firefighter came in to talk about his or her work, then the children were able to play a game on the computer the next day where they identified the different parts of the firefighter's gear and dragged it to the proper place to reinforce their learning from the day before (try *Kids Fireman* iPad app by Ducky Lucky).

Using technology can be the best—and possibly the only way—for you to help children learn about various cultures. Search for different music, games, recipes, photos, and more on the Internet, which has nearly limitless opportunities to help children, and us, understand other people and other lands.

Technology Planning

Planning for the implementation of computer software, app, and Internet use in the early childhood classroom requires an intentional focus on specific learning objectives that are tailored to meet the developmental needs of each child. Think of the computer or mobile device as one of the tools you use to build and enhance learning, and be clear about the purpose each time it is used. Hands-on practice at the computer is important, just as hands-on activities are important in all other areas of the early childhood classroom.

Evaluating Children's Software, Apps, and Websites

A quick scan of Google, iTunes, Amazon, or a look around the software section of your favorite school supply catalog or website will reveal a wide range of commercially available software, websites, and apps designed specifically for young children. The options all sound good, and the ratings from other people are helpful, but how do you know if they are really developmentally appropriate? We're going to give you some guidelines that should help.

We want to help you make good decisions about the software you select, rather than telling you what to use.

You've probably heard the proverb, "Give a man a fish, and you have fed him for today. Teach a man to fish, and you have fed him for a lifetime." We feel the same way about providing a list of software, websites, and apps from which to select. Because new applications come out every day and existing applications are updated frequently, offering specific suggestions will only help for a brief time. As a matter of fact, by the time this book is published, the suggestions are likely to have changed. **We want to help you make good decisions about the software you select, rather than telling you what to use.** This chapter is all about using your good, common sense along with some generally accepted ideas about what makes applications appropriate for young children.

Despite the array of commercial children's software, apps, and websites, there are very few professional resources for evaluating all of this technology. As you might expect, there are many more tools available to assess software for school-age children, but those tools do not always account for the special considerations needed for preschool children. Rather than adapting tools designed for elementary children or leisure applications, we're going to zoom in on what makes software developmentally appropriate for early childhood classroom settings.

Two of the finest examples of software and website evaluation tools designed specifically for early childhood settings are The Haugland/Gerzog Developmental Scale for Web Sites and the Haugland Developmental Software Scale originally published in 1998. These tools are so well structured, they have, for the most part, withstood the test of time. We've adapted them to provide you with guidelines for selecting the software, apps, and websites to use in your classroom. We've also adapted some of the recommendations from an evaluation tool used to assess software on *Children's Technology Review*, a well-respected resource for timely information about the latest developments in children's software, edited by Warren Buckleitner, PhD, a leading authority on children's technology. We've added many of our own recommendations to offer you a unique resource for evaluating early childhood technology applications.

Before we offer our suggestions, we need to define a few terms that are used on the following chart:

- **Software** = By software, we mean applications that are installed on a network or a single computer.
- **Websites =** By websites, we mean places on the Internet that have applications that can be accessed for a fee or at no cost and are designed specifically for children to interact with them. These sites would be examples of cloud computing or software as a service applications (SaaS).
- **Apps =** Apps means interactive software that is operated on a multi-touch mobile device like a smartphone, iPad, or tablet device. Apps are typically smaller, singularly focused experiences.

The Commonsense Approach to Developmentally Appropriate Evaluation of Software, Websites, and Apps Developed for Young Children

ALL Software, Websites, and Apps MUST...	SOME Software, Websites, and Apps SHOULD...	Specifically
Be age appropriate		The activities challenge children without frustrating them and are built upon a sound understanding of the abilities of the suggested age range.
	Allow children to control navigation or the paths they take through the experience	The software responds to the child's on-screen decisions and clicks by allowing a different outcome or path through the experience. Children can move from task to task without adult assistance.
Provide clear on-screen instructions and prompts		For preliterate children, provide verbal instructions or sounds that are prompts. All on-screen written instructions for emerging readers are written simply and clearly and on grade level.
	Offer expanding complexity	Some apps are designed specifically to do one thing and one thing only. Apps for a multi-touch device are often single task. There are some online experiences that offer more complex activities and tasks along with less complex applications.
Allow children to use the software with or without adult guidance		Children should be able to initiate and use the software or website independently.
	Allow children to use it alone or in small groups	
Be free of depictions of violence, sexuality, or other offensive material		No guns, bombs, fighting, or other interactions that cause harm to others or depict graphic sexual activity.
Be free of racist, sexist, or otherwise biased stereotyped graphics, language, or activity		A balance of genders, races, and ethnicities are included, and representations are meaningful to all.

ALL Software, Websites, and Apps MUST...	SOME Software, Websites, and Apps SHOULD...	Specifically
Be process oriented rather than didactic		The material focuses on developing and building upon intrinsic motivation and offers open-ended experiences.
Be "sticky" or engaging and have built-in motivation to stick with it		There are interesting opportunities to interact, with enough feedback and opportunities for additional actions to encourage more interaction.
Offer attractive graphics, animation, and sound but remain uncluttered so children can focus		It should have enough colorful and interesting images and activity to attract and capture interest without overwhelming the senses.
Work consistently, load quickly, and offer a user-friendly and responsive experience		It offers a trouble-free user experience for children.
	Be able to integrate with other devices such as printers, cameras, whiteboards, and multi-touch devices	Not all apps need to print, use photographs, or otherwise work with all devices, but whenever possible, these extensions make the user experience more meaningful and concrete for young children. Having something tangible to take away from the experience whenever possible adds value.
Allow users to freeze or pause and save the application to resume later		Children often have to stop their work or play to do other things. It is extremely frustrating for children to invest time in a computer experience only to lose all of the time invested because they have to stop their play.
	Make objects and situations change or transform	Much of the value of online and computer experiences comes from making things happen and navigating simulations that change depending on the choices the users make.
	Accommodate dual language learners (DLLs)	It offers a variety of online experiences and tools in the languages of the specific dual language learners (DLLs) in your program.

ALL Software, Websites, and Apps MUST...	SOME Software, Websites, and Apps SHOULD...	Specifically
	Accommodate atypically developing children and those with disabilities	It provides online tools or adaptive devices that allow children with disabilities or special needs to use technology purposefully and meaningfully.
Be self-correcting or provide meaningful feedback		Online systems and tools and other computer software and apps should respond to children as they use them. Responses can be neutral, corrective, or encouraging. For example, when children click "submit," they proceed to the next screen (neutral). If they successfully add a piece to an electronic puzzle, it fits and responds with a sound that indicates that it worked (encouraging). If a child tries to match a triangle with a circle in an online matching game, the system will not allow the action, responds with audible correction ("That didn't work. Try again."), and may ultimately offer a hint or correction (corrective).
Be free of commercial messages, marketing, up-sells, or in-app purchases		Applications should not entice children to click on links to online stores or otherwise suggest additional purchases.
Offer experiences that help children learn and meet curriculum objectives		Carefully evaluate the objectives and goals of the online applications and software and align them with those embedded in your curriculum and/or your state standards, including the all-important social and emotional objectives.
Be a valuable use of time		The materials provide a range of educationally sound online applications that nurture cognitive, physical, social, and emotional development and stimulate divergent and creative thinking so children's time is used well.

ALL Software, Websites, and Apps MUST...	SOME Software, Websites, and Apps SHOULD...	Specifically
Encourage divergent thinking and offer divergent paths to explore		Applications should offer more than one right answer or linear path to follow. Making different choices yields different responses and situations.
	Encourage creativity	Online or computer experiences allow children to virtually replicate creative play like art, blocks, dramatic play, creating or completing stories, and other creative explorations.
Children can select the level of challenge with which they are comfortable		Children should be able to adjust the settings so they can increase or decrease the difficulty of the experience. The goal is to intrinsically motivate children to get to the next level or increase the challenge, but also allow them to avoid frustration.
Is built on meaningful, relevant, and interesting themes or plots		Young children respond and learn best from situations that make sense to them. Plot-oriented software should always be grounded in experiences that are familiar and relevant to young children.
	Record children's progress to offer opportunities for self-regulation, as well as to inform teachers	The software and applications should track children's progress and graphically depict the progress for children, teachers, and parents.
Informs emergent curriculum or future planning for individualization		Information gathered through observation of children and/or the progress tracking embedded in the application is used to plan for the group and for individual children.
Have sounds that can be adjusted or turned off		For some children, sounds can be distracting or overwhelming, and for others, encouraging and engaging.
Balances cost with function		The price reflects the amount of use that can be expected as well as the depth or flexibility of the app, software, or online subscription.

Using Software, Apps, and Online Systems Developed for Use by Adults

We've offered suggestions about how to think about the commercially offered technology programs available for children, and the range of these applications you might provide in your commonsense digital classroom. However, the options are not limited to software designed for children. You may already have desktop applications and apps on your computer or tablet that you can use with children for open-ended, creative, and divergent activities. There are even a few websites for specific tasks that can be used with guidance from a teacher. Using these tools might take a little out-of-the-box thinking and supervision on your part, but they can offer very rich experiences. Here are a few examples to stimulate your thinking:

A Few Ideas About How to Use Software, Apps, and Online Systems Developed for Adults in Open-Ended Classroom Projects and Experiences for Children

Type of Software, App, or Online System	Example of a Few Brand Names	A Few Possible Uses
Word Processing	Word, WordPerfect, OpenOffice, Google Docs, Pages	Group or individual experiences with adult help at first, and without assistance later • Language experience stories • Child-created recipes • Classroom-created books, posters, signs, letters, newsletters • Dictated descriptions for drawings and other creations
Spreadsheets	Excel, OpenOffice, Google Docs, Numbers	Group or individual experiences with adult help • Simple classroom graphs that expand as children add responses • Charts for classroom routines and jobs • Calendars
Presentation	PowerPoint, Keynote, Prezi, SlideRocket	Group or individual experiences with adult help at first, and without assistance later • Easy graphics of all kinds • Child-created signs • Slideshows of photos and drawings from field trips and special projects • Sequential steps for children to follow to create a recipe, set up snack time, or complete a task

Type of Software, App, or Online System	Example of a Few Brand Names	A Few Possible Uses
Email	Outlook, Apple Mail, Gmail, Yahoo	Group or individual experiences with adult help at first, and without assistance later, but careful monitoring is required because this is an activity that takes place on the Internet • Pen pals • Thank-you notes • Birthday and holiday wishes • Keeping in touch with classroom members who move or are absent for extended periods
Image and Photo Editing	Photoshop Elements, Paint, Pixelmator, Picasa	Individual experiences with adult help at first, and without assistance later • Creating drawings and digital paintings • Using filters and color options to transform scanned images or photos • Making photos larger or smaller to print out or use in other projects
Online Photo Sharing	Picasa, Flickr, iPhoto	Group or individual experiences with adult help at first, and without assistance later, but careful monitoring is required because this is an activity that takes place on the Internet • Creating and sharing online galleries of scanned images or photos for class art shows • Sharing images of field trips and special projects with parents as they happen, using cameras and smart devices to send images on the spot • Categorizing images by color, shape, style, subject matter, or other attribute
Online Video Sharing	YouTube, Vimeo	Group or individual experiences with adult help • Creating and sharing videos created in class or on field trips with parents as they happen, using video cameras and smart devices to send images on the spot
Video chat or video conferencing	Skype, Google Chat, AIM	Individual or group experiences with adult help • Keeping in touch with classroom members who move or are absent for extended periods • Having experts make presentations about their careers or special talents using web cams instead of coming into the classroom • Connecting with family members who are deployed for the military or are away on other trips • Virtual field trips

Technology for Dual Language Learners (DLLs), Point #2

Guidance from key researchers and national organizations has made it clear that young DLLs need learning experiences that support their home language as well as English. The first question teachers ask regarding software to support their work with children who are dual language learners is whether to use translation programs. The answer to this question is yes and no. On one hand, the availability of computer and Internet resources for translating words and documents has changed the ability of early childhood professionals to teach diverse groups of students. On the other hand, the problems with those programs make them difficult and sometimes risky to use.

There are some significant advantages to having Internet access and translation software. Better than a bilingual dictionary, many translation programs provide sound so you can hear correct pronunciations. You can find many languages instantly. And many programs will not only translate the words but also will help you to construct sentences.

The concern about using these programs is that most of them have been developed for use by businesses or travelers. They don't use forms of words—like *lavatory*—that would be appropriate for young children; they don't anticipate shades of meaning needed in different circumstances; and they don't account for slang. Also, keep in mind that there may be many versions or dialects of a language, and the program you choose may use words from one region that are not recognized in another region. For important documents such as parent agreements or child observation notes, it's important to get at least two native speakers to read the translation. No assessment is valid if it is translated into a language for which it has not been validated—so avoid using translation software for formal assessment or diagnostic purposes. When using translation software as one part of your DLL toolbox, make sure that you add graphics, pictures, or gestures to clarify your meaning.

Beyond the issue of specifically designed translators, there is a wealth of material available online in different languages that may not be accessible in any other way. Even if you can't afford to purchase stories, games, videos, and activities for all the languages you need, many of those things can be provided via the Internet. While we don't recommend letting the computer become the teacher, you can certainly use these software resources and join in the learning with the children.

Assistive Technology for Children with Special Needs, Point #2

There are a number of programs that you can purchase or access on websites that have been designed specifically to help children develop particular skills that are likely to be found in individualized education plans (IEPs). It is important to keep in mind that goals for children with special needs are most effective when embedded in real-life, everyday functions. Computer-based activities, however, can help you get started with practice on very specialized tasks that can then be practiced during regular activities in the classroom. For example, a computer activity that requires the child to click the mouse or touch the screen to pop bubbles that appear at different locations would help the child build fine motor skills. Re-creating the same type of action with a table game or outdoors with real bubbles would be a valuable follow-up.

Websites like www.voki.com or http://blabberize.com were not intended as speech therapy supports, but they provide multiple ways for you to work with children who have speech and language delays or disabilities. You can create characters or use digital photos you have on your computer and record the child's voice—making it look and sound different. The results are so funny that even children who are very hesitant may be encouraged to practice their oral language, and their results can be recorded for your records.

One type of software that can be helpful for children with special needs and for children who speak other languages is picture communication board software. This software is available from a variety of sources and will enable you to design and print a set of pictures that can be posted on a board or other format so children can point to the picture in order to make their thoughts understood.

SAMPLE TECHNOLOGY LESSON PLAN # 2:
LEARNING ABOUT COMPUTER GAMES

Purpose

To engage children in playing computer games that accurately and appropriately serve a purpose in helping them meet the learning goals you have set for them, while also developing their understanding of software and applications

Target ages

This flexible activity can be adapted for any age over 18 months and individualized for each child.

Learning objectives

- Language arts and literacy: Children will learn more sophisticated tier-two words in the context of math skills games.
- Math: Children will understand how to use math skills such as counting, adding, subtracting, and spatial reasoning with the two-dimensional screen.
- Social and emotional: Children will practice focus, attention, and self-regulation while complying with the parameters of math skills computer games.

Keywords

app	icon	math words that are	restart
application	loading	part of the	screen
back	log in	selected game,	software
click	log out	such as *plus,*	window
drag		*minus, rotate,* and	
		match	

Preparation

Before the activity, select one computer math game or app (such as *Park Math* or *Bug Math* for the iPad/iPod that allow the child to choose counting activities or more advanced adding and subtracting activities) that has multiple levels of challenge or several games that address similar skills. Make sure that each child in your group will be able to participate in a computer game and learn the concepts they need in math.

Materials

Print a grid with the keywords for this activity and a column for each child. This will be your Children's Software Checklist (see the table that follows this lesson plan).
Make a short list of other manipulatives or learning materials you have in the classroom that might teach the same concepts you are highlighting with this computer game.

Activity

Make a note in your lesson plans to play the selected math game with a few of the children each day until they have all had an opportunity. Some children might choose to play on the computer during choice time. Others might have to be brought over during small-group time or some other time during the day.

As each child attempts to play the math game, discuss the appropriate keywords with him or her, and mark your checklist to show that you used these words with the child. While playing, they are learning how software works as well as learning the math skills, vocabulary, and game-playing strategies mentioned in the objectives.

After you have worked with a child on the computer math game, you will be prepared to reinforce the math learning he or she experienced by highlighting the same skills during play with three-dimensional objects in the classroom (as you have listed).

Children's Software Checklist									
	Sue	Joe	Sun	Paz	Kim	Ben	José	JP	Ed
Log in									
Log out									
Window									
Click									
Drag									
Insert									
Add									
More									
Total									

411 FOR DIRECTORS AND OTHER ADMINISTRATORS: SOFTWARE, APPS, AND WEBSITE ACTIVITIES

Important Considerations

How to balance cost, need, and expected use

You may wonder how many packaged software, apps, and or Internet services your staff will maintain, monitor, and really use, and whether your program can afford it all. For all practical purposes, it is possible to have an engaging technology program with very few additional commercially available software programs developed specifically for children. How? With ingenuity, it is possible to offer meaningful creative, divergent, and engaging experiences for young children using only software originally designed for business, productivity, and lifestyle use. If you add in scanners, digital cameras, printers, Internet access, and well-trained creative staff members, your program can be technology-rich without too many packaged applications. However, at the very least, you will want to take advantage of some of the free high-quality Internet systems offered specifically for preschool children like PBS Kid's Island, Sesame Street Games, and National Geographic's Little Kids. Using inexpensive, yet highly engaging apps like those suggested in Children's Technology Review will be a very affordable alternative to some of the more expensive applications. Nonetheless, the opportunities offered by the many desktop and SaaS software for children, and the applications used with interactive whiteboards and multi-touch tables, may be too powerful and too engaging to ignore.

This is really a function of your budget, the cost for the applications, how much the applications will be used, how the applications fit into the curriculum, and the likelihood that they have staying power. Costs range dramatically from free to very expensive.

Finding and purchasing the most developmentally appropriate and meaningful programs

Finding applications that meet all of the criteria in our commonsense list on pages 59–62 will be difficult, if not impossible, but many titles will meet most of the criteria. Just be sure to provide software that is inclusive of all of the children in your program, and aim to find software that meets many of the objectives of the standards in your state or in your curricula.

Ask the following questions about children's software, sites, and apps:

- Does it meet most of the criteria for developmental appropriateness?
- Are the staff and children likely to use it often and purposely?
- Will the staff have the appropriate level of technology awareness and skills to use it well?
- Is the overall variety of programs diverse enough, or is there an abundance of programs that support one skill/concept/content area and too few that support others?
- Do I have the budget to support the cost and the professional development needed to support its use?
- Will I have to pay to upgrade the application?
- What do the reviews from other users say?
- Why is it a good fit for my program?
- Will it help my staff members meet their objectives?
- Can it be used for multiple age groups and shared among the staff members on multiple machines?
- What other peripherals, devices, or other applications will I need to make it work?
- Is there built-in technical support?
- Is hands-on training needed, and if so, how much will it cost?
- Is your program set up to support and monitor its use?
- Is it safe?

Interactive Whiteboards and Multi-Touch Table Devices

6

Miss Mei-Lin's class of five-year-olds has children who speak four different languages. She has created an activity for her multi-touch table by adapting a popular learning game so the children can play in pairs and select cues in the language they want to use. She then assigns "language buddies" so each child partners with someone who speaks his language. The pairs can play the game together, playing off his combined talents and building their conversation skills in both English and their shared language. The game adapted by Miss Mei-Lin asks the children to select an icon representing their language as they begin the game. For example, children on one side of the table could select Mandarin, and children on the other side could select English. The activity might require children to quickly gather letters from all over the board, making it better for two children to cooperate rather than compete. The game gives the prompts in Mandarin or English, depending upon whose turn it is.

An interactive whiteboard (IWB) is a large wall-mounted or free-standing screen that works like a huge computer monitor with touch-screen functionality. Multi-touch tables engage children in similar interactivity, but instead of a wall-mounted screen, the display is on a table at a comfortable height for children to stand around and make things happen. This chapter will describe the IWBs first, then cover multi-touch tables and conclude with guidance applicable to both.

Let's start with an important explanation. What do we mean by multi-touch? You may already be familiar with trackpads or screens that can react to touch—for example, you may use a touch-screen computer when you withdraw money with your ATM card. However, with that technology, you only use one finger to touch one thing at a time. Multi-touch technology, on the other hand, has created an explosion of creative and practical ways to interact with and control what the computer is doing. A multi-touch trackpad or screen can detect more than one point of touch and use that information in different ways. You may have seen people with iPhones pinch an image to make it smaller, or people with multi-touch trackpads on their laptop computers using one finger to tap on a selection, two fingers to rotate an image, three fingers to swipe to a different window, and so on. Interactive whiteboards (IWBs) and tables, as well as tablets and some smartphones, use this technology so that most of what happens on the screen is controlled by the fluid movements of your fingers.

IWBs take the multi-touch experience to a higher level by offering software designed to support learning and exploring. Images can be dragged, circled, enlarged, cropped, hidden, duplicated, sorted, and changed, all with the movement of your fingers on the board. Even more amazing, multi-touch tables are developed to accept touch from up to eight users, to recognize which person is which, and to track their movements individually. The software available for IWBs and multi-touch tables is designed to make maximum use of these touch capabilities in developmentally appropriate ways.

Interactive Whiteboards (IWBs)

The first thing you may notice about an interactive whiteboard is that it is big. It almost seems out of place in a preschool classroom where everything seems so small. The IWB may have a diagonal measurement anywhere from four feet to nine feet. Several companies produce the equipment and the software to run it, and there are some important differences. It is a bit confusing because there is a low-tech classroom item called a whiteboard—the shiny white surface that allows you to write with colored markers and then wipe clean. Some people say *whiteboard* when they really mean the high-tech IWB. Others call their IWB by the product name from the manufacturer, such as Promethean or Smartboard. Some IWBs are actually operated by way of an image that comes from a projector and the responsiveness to touch that comes from infrared detection. What this means to you is this type of IWB is portable. Anywhere you can hook up the projector and computer, you can project onto a smooth surface and create a new interactive whiteboard. Other versions contain all of the electronics within the board itself, so you purchase the actual IWB and software, but no projector is needed.

A computer controls how the IWB functions. If the computer is connected to the Internet, then web-based software and search results can be part of the IWB experience. Depending on the version, you may be able to simulate the writing experience on the IWB with digital or infrared pens—or in many cases you can write on the screen with your fingers and use the software to recognize, enhance, or save what you wrote. It is not necessary to have the IWB's computer connected to the Internet, but that certainly adds depth and versatility to the activities you are able to create.

So, is the IWB just a really big board that lights up and lets you and the children write on it? The educational value of the IWB is revealed when used by a teacher who has learned to take advantage of its many unique and impressive features. Your IWB will come with software—and often with training from the supplier. If you have the time and the motivation, you will be able to learn to create some amazing, developmentally appropriate learning experiences for your students with the new software and with programs that are already familiar to you. Take the time to learn and plan ahead to use the special features of the IWB. With practice and confidence, you will find many ways to express your creativity. Some of the features that make the interactive whiteboard such an exciting technology for early childhood educators include the ability to:

1. Plan activities, displays, and demonstrations in advance, then play them as needed, while being able to manipulate and highlight them as needed.
2. Download images and information from the Internet and insert them into a presentation or activity.
3. Create stories and illustrations with the children using your own digital photos or images from the Internet—with the ability to crop, move, and alter the photos as well.
4. Let the children touch the screen to move images, such as moving pictures from one circle to another to sort them or create patterns.
5. Save the work and activities that are being worked on.

6. Display children's journal entries or stories to practice reading to the whole group, and to highlight and illustrate an entry or a story on the spot.

7. Have more sophisticated graphing with sounds, pictures, and comparisons that can't happen with paper charts.

8. Interact with, act out, or reorganize pages or chapters of a story.

9. Create podcasts.

10. Develop learning games and puzzles that are tailored to the learning needs and current interests of the children.

11. Create activities, then translate them into the languages needed by the children at the time.

12. Explore informative websites, videos, and activities on a large scale right in the middle of any activity.

13. Use the computer right from the large screen while you have the children's attention, instead of having to disconnect from their attention while you look something up on the small screen.

Multi-Touch Tables

Now, imagine being able to do all of these things, but instead of a large screen against the wall, they happen on the surface of a table that is just the right height for young children. The tabletop version of the interactive whiteboard (IWB) is called a multi-touch table. At this writing, there is only one company that makes a multi-touch table for preschool classrooms, but these tables are available for adults as well, so more options for preschool may be coming soon. SMART Table is the name of the multi-touch table that is currently available for preschool, and it can be ordered from several different early childhood education supply catalogs. The currently available table format is referred to as a multi-touch, because one person can use different types of touch (swipe, drag, tap, double tap, and so on) to make things happen on the screen, and because up to eight people can touch the screen at the same time.

But wait, there's more! Multi-touch tables also come with software that makes it easy for you to program your own games, activities, and lessons for the table. You can also purchase software for activities to use on the table, or download packages that have been developed by other teachers like you. Like the IWBs, the table can be connected to the Internet to download and use almost anything available. The screen on the table is not as big as an IWB and allows children to gather around and work alone or together with a manageable surface area, and they can reach all of it. The images on the table are bright and crisp. The sound quality is excellent.

This technology is currently very expensive—generally more costly than IWBs. Whether it is worth the investment depends entirely on how much training the user gets and how confident he or she will be in creating activities that make the best use of its capabilities. Spending thousands of dollars just to make it possible for children to move squares to one side and circles to the other side of the screen is certainly not developmentally appropriate or financially appropriate—even if the shapes are brightly colored and accompanied by bells and whistles. The following list highlights some of the functionality that sets multi-touch tables apart from other kinds of preschool equipment and technology:

1. Children can work together over a table where everything is in reach.
2. The teacher can actually design applications that match her goals to student abilities and interests.
3. Access to the Internet can be provided at the table so children can use the touch-screen technology to explore and learn from the Web.
4. Unlike the IWBs, multi-touch tables track each child's actions from their position around the table and can collect that information to form learning portfolios.
5. Activities combined with voice prompts can increase interactivity and discussion around the board.
6. Voice prompts can be recorded in the languages of the children.
7. Some programs can actually record the voices of the children around the table and collect those recordings to add to learning portfolios.
8. Programs can be designed to respond to the child's accomplishments, so the activity can change as the child develops more skills.
9. Activities can be saved and re-opened for extended learning and table-based projects.
10. Music, sounds, and animation can increase student engagement.
11. Working around the table can foster collaborative play and exploration and allow abler children to learn alongside children who are not as advanced cognitively or linguistically.
12. Using the Internet and digital photographs, activities can be designed around the children's actual community, classroom, families, field trips, and interests.

Interactive whiteboards (IWBs) and multi-touch tables, such as the SMART Table, may cost considerably more than classroom computers and other technology devices because of their level of sophistication. This cost and this complexity make these devices impractical for many programs. They can, however, add extraordinary richness and depth to preschool and kindergarten learning. Now, here are some examples of activities that can be used to meet learning objectives in a preschool or kindergarten classroom:

Activity Examples

- Scan in the pictures from the pages of a popular story so the children have to put them in the correct order to show they understood the story.

- Keep a running graph, such as a graph of how many children are wearing long sleeves, then save and go back to it, adding new information and talking about how the graph changes with the seasons.

- Check out websites in advance, and post the links so you know exactly what you'll see when you explore the websites with the children.

- Open a website and then circle key items or write notes on the screen.

- Practice more realistic sorting by showing a photo of a kitchen and the foods that were brought home from the grocery store, and sort them by dragging the cold things into the refrigerator.

- Explore websites of teaching ideas submitted by teachers, provided by the manufacturers of these devices, and try out these ideas in your own classroom.

- Show a video and stop before the end—let the children guess or draw or select images that they think will be the end of the story.

- Show the words—and accompanying pictures—of songs and rhymes, while singing them.

- Use the features to create active games—such as memory or concentration games—that include active elements.

- Work with children to design spaces and plan activities. For example, create a map of your classroom, and discuss how some things might be rearranged.

- Facilitate exploring with activities that ask children to find and uncover things, put things together, and rearrange things.

- Use illustrations from books to separate the elements of the picture into usable pieces to make new stories or problems to solve.

- Embed links to the Internet for on-the-spot investigations. For example, after showing the book *Rosie's Walk*, when the child touches the fox, a link takes him or her to a YouTube video showing how foxes live and eat.

Features of Interactive Touch-Screen Devices

	Interactive Whiteboards	Multi-Touch Tables	Tablets, iPad
Accommodates large and small groups	X	X	1–2 children
Requires projector and screen or white space	X		Can be attached to LCD projector for group viewing
Allows teachers to program applications		X	Not easily
Can use any program or software	X		Only those designed for the specific operating system
Can be used outdoors, on field trips, or anywhere at any time without power			X
Operating system	Windows or Mac	Device specific	Windows or Mac compatible
Internet capable	X	X	X
Price range	$$$$	$$$$	$$
Ease of use	Specialized training required	Specialized training required	Easy to use
Impact and educational potential	Huge	Huge	Huge

Technology for Dual Language Learners (DLLs), Point #3

Interactive whiteboards (IWBs) and multi-touch tables offer some especially interesting capabilities for children who are DLLs. Any work they perform on the IWB can be saved. The multi-touch table can even record what they are saying as they are playing. And because you design and control the activities with a computer, you can add, subtract, and combine any languages you need at any given time. This kind of responsiveness gives children who speak other languages access to content learning in their home language while they are also learning English. It also makes it possible for two children who speak different languages to participate together or even collaborate on an activity that has cues or prompts in each of their languages.

Assistive Technology for Children with Special Needs, Point #3

The IWB and multi-touch surfaces provide a wonderful introduction to the use of technology, for children who need a larger visual field or larger movements to be able to interact. Children can practice important skills and learn content in the larger, more responsive multi-touch format. The large size and collaborative activities make it possible for children to work together, combining their abilities and learning with and from each other. You can create and modify activities to precisely address your objectives for each child and allow the children to show what they know and can do accordingly.

SAMPLE TECHNOLOGY LESSON PLAN #3:
SEEK AND FIND YOUR FRIENDS GAME

Purpose
Using familiar people, this game offers practice in using the multi-touch surface while addressing content from learning objectives.

Target ages
This flexible activity can be adapted for any age over 18 months and individualized for each child.

Learning objectives
- Language arts and literacy: Children will learn letter recognition and reading names.
- Logical reasoning: Children will learn about comparing, remembering, and matching.
- Math: Children will learn shape recognition.

Keywords

circle	drag	oval	square
diamond	match	reveal	triangle

Preparation
Use full-body digital photos of each child in the classroom. Create an activity in the software for your device that uses the name of each child, the photo of each child, and pieces of the photos. Create the game so that each child will see a shape with her own name, move it to find the photo or name of her friend, and then find the friend's head and match it to the full-body picture, the shoes, and so on.

Materials
Print out these photos and cut them into puzzle shapes that will allow the children to practice the same activity away from the board or bring the puzzle shapes home.

Activity
Each child finds the shape with his or her name, moves the shape, and reveals the name or photo of a friend. This can be a memory game where the children find the name under one shape and then find the full or partial photos under other shapes. It can also be a matching game where the children drag the parts of the photo onto the whole photo, or it can be a reading game where the children read the name and then find the right photo.

Mobile Devices— Multi-Touch Tablets and Smartphones

7

Teacher Trina was fortunate enough to receive a small grant that enabled her to buy multi-touch tablet devices for her preschool classroom. Several children in her class have diagnosed speech and language delays, so her first project was teaching all the children how to use an app that allowed them to record their own speech and hear it back in funny ways. She knew she was right on the mark when she saw that even the most hesitant child tried different word sounds and giggled at the result he was able to achieve on his own. The children with individualized education plans (IEPs) were able to practice the functional goal of pronouncing initial consonant sounds out loud, and all of the children were able to practice phonemic awareness as part of their language arts/literacy goal.

Mobile devices are actually small computers that we carry around to keep and get information, perform applications, and sometimes even make phone calls. Some examples are tablets, iPads, Androids, iPod Touch, Kindle Fire, and smartphones. Some e-book readers also have the ability to connect with the Internet or handle email, so they are part of this category as well. In this chapter, we will focus on how to use the kinds of devices that teachers and parents are giving to preschoolers, and how to use these devices to support real learning in developmentally appropriate ways.

Mobile devices have special features that make them especially attractive to—and useful for—young children. They are shiny, have lots of buttons, and respond to touch with interesting graphics and cool sounds. Who wouldn't love that? The features that have made these devices so popular with adults are also attractive for young children as well. In fact, if you have one of these devices and you have a young child, you may have a hard time keeping them apart. Here are some of the key features of mobile devices (a device may have all or some of the features):

- Handheld—even a toddler can hold and control it
- Powerful—within the small device is the power to access the Internet as well as many apps that are specially designed for the device
- New—these devices haven't been around for very long, and their newness makes them all the more enticing
- Mobile—not only can you hold it in your hand, but you can also move around wherever you want without wires or cords to tie you down
- Changing—new apps, new devices, and new features are coming out every day
- Battery life—a compelling feature is that these devices have a long battery life— no need to run for a charger every few hours
- Cameras—most can take pictures and video and even let you have a video chat with someone on another device
- Microphone—most let you record things for the children or record the children's own words, songs, or stories
- Sound—many also have speakers so you can play music or recorded messages without hooking up to bulky speakers
- No moving parts—nothing to push in or pull out, few switches or buttons— almost all the action takes place by touching the screen so there's nothing to lose or break (except the device itself)
- Covers—there are many different cases, covers, and frames available to protect your investment
- Motion—internal gyroscopes make it possible for the screen to change when you tip or move the device so it always faces you

- Movement—respond to tilting, shaking—even jumping up and down—a great feature for preschool hands-on learning
- Quick and easy—easy to start, easy to understand, and easy to open whenever you want to use them

Handheld mobile devices are quick to start, easy to use, and intuitively designed. When they are charged overnight, they can last all day without a cord, and you can get to the Internet or an application in the blink of an eye. Many choices are available with one click on a recognizable icon. If needed, a click brings up the on-screen keyboard, allowing you to type words for documents, searches, emails, and text messages. These features give them a strong advantage over laptop or desktop computers, and their size makes it possible to include one in any or all interest areas in your classroom—something you wouldn't do with a laptop.

Toddlers and preschoolers are able to open a handheld device, navigate around to find activities, select an activity, enjoy it, and find another with little help from adults. For example, the iPad app from Sesame Street Workshop called *Elmo's Monstermaker* uses Elmo to provide spoken cues that prompt children to pick one of the monsters and then select things to add—eyes, nose, mouth, and hat. Once the child has designed his or her monster, he or she can then choose to make the monster dance to different types of music, play a game with Elmo, or pose for a picture. If the child clicks on the camera, the picture will be saved for later viewing or sharing and can be printed as well. All of this can be managed by a toddler or preschooler with no help from an adult.

Not all apps are as developmentally appropriate for young children. You will need to view and try every app and website before making it accessible on the device. Avoid apps that have advertising or in-app sales (where a window pops up in the middle of an activity, asking you to click to purchase something). Here is a list of other things to avoid:

- Any activity that is just a two-dimensional, inauthentic, weak replacement for activities that are better done in real life
- Apps that act like simple, boring flash cards
- One-dimensional activities that are uninspiring and offer no challenge or choice
- Apps that do things for the child instead of encouraging independent actions
- Devices or apps that are too slow or too complicated
- Coloring pages
- Apps that are really just opportunities to market a show or product

In general, if you wouldn't offer a similar corresponding traditional activity (like worksheets or flash cards), that app is inappropriate. This is where your common sense is the best first lens for making selections.

A few examples of mobile handheld, multi-touch activities that would be developmentally appropriate are as follows:

- Apps that turn the device into a musical instrument to shake, pluck, or strum
- Learning games that invite the child to jump up and down a certain number of times to indicate the answer
- Apps that create playlists of songs to enhance a certain topic or theme
- Sending the device home loaded with activities to extend learning
- Translation programs that allow you to say a word and have it translated, or that speak the translation so you can hear the proper pronunciation
- Apps that allow free drawing and painting with different tools, colors, and media
- Storybook apps that let children control the pace and sequence of a story and do some activities while listening, such as The Monster at the End of This Book app that reads the story to you and asks you to turn pages, knock things down, or open doors as you participate in the story
- Bilingual storybook apps
- Apps such as SmackTalk! that record the child's voice and play it back with funny sounds, which encourages all children, especially dual language learners (DLLs) or children with speech or language delays, because it supports their practice of oral speech through interacting with a fun activity where they don't feel the pressure of the therapist trying to get them to speak
- Apps such as Babies that support social and emotional development by showing photos of faces in different expressions so you can talk about how the babies are feeling
- Apps such as Zoodle for Android that allow you to register each child with his age and interests, and the software will keep track of their ages and send games and activities periodically to match their interests, skills, and developmental stage

Some things teachers can do with mobile devices:

- Create podcasts by recording video and/or sound on your mobile device to capture a story or activity that you record for children to listen to or bring home.
- Help children create podcasts with video and/or sound that the children record as they practice stories or skits.

- Record verbal safety instructions for fire drills, lockdowns, and field trips in different languages, and play them to be sure dual language learners (DLLs) understand.
- Take pictures of class activities or field trips, and upload them to your program's website.

The number of choices in the handheld device market is growing rapidly. One factor to consider as you decide what to use is that some products work well with others and some don't integrate with any other product. For example, Apple products are compatible with each other and use iTunes as an online store to order and pay for music, apps, audiobooks, movies, and podcasts. iPads, iPod Touches, and iPhones can all be updated, stocked, and managed using the free iTunes software. iTunes software can be downloaded from the Internet onto any type of computer for no charge, and anyone can get iTunes and use it on any kind of computer to organize the music they have or download new music. You can load all of your CDs into your computer, and the music will be stored in an organized, searchable format. If you decide to purchase an Android or other similarly designed mobile device, you can download the Android Market software to your desktop or laptop computer to function similarly to iTunes in the storage of material. These programs require you to set up an account connected to a credit card, which will be billed anytime you order something, although some teachers and directors purchase gift cards that can be used to make purchases on these sites without having to divulge your personal credit card information. There are a lot of free apps available for both kinds of devices. Keep in mind that free is not always best. Reading the reviews at sites such as http://childrenstech.com or http://ecetech.net will help you make selections to meet your needs.

Developmentally Appropriate Activities for Preschool/Kindergarten

As children get more adept at making things happen on tablets and smaller handheld devices, the possibilities explode. Not only can they access the Internet and use the devices to record their voices and take pictures and video, but there are so many more kinds of learning that can happen with these easy-to-use examples of technology. Much of what we presented about choosing and using software in Chapter 5 applies to handheld devices, too. The following are some activities specifically for handheld multi-touch devices that can help children accomplish important learning objectives.

Logic and Reasoning: Look for activities that promote decision-making and problem-solving skills. Children can take an increasing amount of control in determining which activity they will do and what options they will choose. Activities that ask children to anticipate what might happen and choose accordingly are great for this kind of thinking. Also, look for activities that provide parts that have to be "assembled" on the screen.

Thinking and Learning: Curiosity and perseverance are two qualities that can be supported by the more sophisticated apps available for young children. Mobile devices can also be used to explore interesting websites, such as the NASA website or a car repair website. One iPad app allows you to create virtual cupcakes by selecting from an array of batter flavors and decorative cups, setting the timer and waiting for it to ding, pulling out the pan, and shaking the iPad to get the cakes out, selecting icings and toppings and even candles, and then tapping your creation a number of times to see bites taken out of it. You can even save pictures of your favorites. Of course, this activity will be even more meaningful if you have already baked real cupcakes with the children before having this virtual experience.

Math: Ignore simple counting and sorting activities, and look for math activities with different levels of difficulty and games that relate to how math is used in real life. Repeating the word *triangle* over and over is not likely to have much educational value. Dragging a triangle shape onto a photo of a slice of pizza connects the meaning of what a triangle is to something young children might know and understand. Finding complex shapes and anticipating how they might fit together to make a pizza, a glass of milk, or an apple would be even more practical. Counting how many virtual slices of pepperoni will fit on your slice of pizza adds another dimension to a math activity that is portable and independent for the child who is ready for it.

Science: There are many software programs available to support science learning for young children. Keep in mind that children need tools to conduct and record observations and also to look up information as they learn about living things, inanimate objects, principles of physics, and environmental science. With a handheld device on the playground, a child can use the camera to take pictures of plants growing in the yard, look them up on the Internet to find out what they are, then drag the photos into a storymaking app that can be added to as the season progresses.

Creative Arts: In addition to the many drawing and painting apps, there are also apps that duplicate the familiar Etch A Sketch activity. There are apps that enable you to work with a child to design and create objects, machines, and clothes. Tablets or iPhones can also be used as musical instruments that often have surprisingly great sound and realistic action.

Language Arts and Literacy: Handheld devices add to language arts and literacy activities by providing apps that are available in the languages that reflect the needs of your group. There are apps that encourage the learning of writing right on the screen with feedback and fun interactive activities. Of course, we have already described story-reading apps and using a handheld device as an e-book reader, but these devices also allow children to play with word sounds or write and record their own stories.

Social Studies: There is a wealth of possibilities on the Internet to help children explore and learn about the people in their school, their family, and their community. You can also find pictures, recipes, music, and games from other cultures. You can bring portable devices with you on neighborhood walks to take pictures of buildings and people in your environment, and work with the children to turn them into games and puzzles for your classroom.

Technology for Dual Language Learners (DLLs), Point #4

Handheld multi-touch devices can be invaluable in an environment where multiple languages are spoken. You will certainly appreciate being able to hear spoken translations of keywords at your fingertips. Just be sure to check reviews of translation apps and websites before depending on them.

With no wires and a long battery life, these devices can be dependable communication aids—allowing you to find pictures or short videos to illustrate the points you are trying to communicate to children who are DLLs or their families. Bilingual apps such as bilingual storybooks or songs in two languages can help in three ways:
1. They provide portable, accessible support to each child in his or her home language.
2. They help the child learn connections between his or her first and second languages.
3. They can help you, the teacher, learn words and phrases in each child's language, too!

Assistive Technology for Children with Special Needs, Point #4

Their portability and versatility make multi-touch tablet computers very useful in an inclusive classroom. They can be turned on quickly to use pictures or graphic organizers to help you and a child who has speech or language delays to communicate. There are voice apps that will pronounce a word that is written or selected from a list. You can customize lists for each child, each part of the day, or each activity.

The multi-touch capabilities of many tablets allow children to participate in activities even if they don't have the fine motor coordination to tap a small icon on the screen. Many activities are activated by shaking, tilting, or rotating the device.

SAMPLE TECHNOLOGY LESSON PLAN #4:
WORKING WITH SOUNDS AND WORDS

Purpose
To use a voice-recording app on a handheld device to help children practice pronouncing letter sounds and words

Target ages
This flexible activity can be adapted for any age over 18 months and individualized for each child.

Learning objectives
- Language arts and literacy: Children will learn phonemic awareness, listening skills , and oral language skills.
- Science: Children will use their sense of hearing to observe and compare changes in voice sounds.

Keywords

app	load	slow	tap
back	low	speed	volume
fast	play	stop	
high	record	swipe	

Preparation

Download a voice recording and modification app, such as SmackTalk! or Voices to the devices that the children will use.

Materials

handheld multi-touch devices that have sound-recording and playback capabilities

Activity

These apps allow children to record their voices saying a sound, word, or sentence, and then modifying it with special effects and playing it back as if the child's words are being spoken by a cute animal or unusual character. Originally designed to provide entertainment, the silliness of the results of these modified recordings is very motivating to young children for practicing speaking and listening skills. Show the child how the app works. Allow the child to select from the options and then experiment independently. Toddlers will be encouraged to practice making sounds and attempting words along with you. Preschoolers will be able to see the effects of their pronunciation, pitch, and volume and, with your collaboration, will be able to practice troublesome words to see if they can get the playback to sound clearer. Kindergartners can play a game using cue cards that they have to read into the recorder for funny results.

411 FOR DIRECTORS AND OTHER ADMINISTRATORS: MOBILE DEVICES—MULTI-TOUCH TABLETS AND SMARTPHONES

Multi-touch devices, smartphones, iPads, and other tablet computers may very well be the most important and revolutionary development to impact education in more than a century. They have the power to completely revolutionize how children learn and how teachers offer learning experiences. They might, in fact, be education's version of the greatest invention since sliced bread, due to the enormous potential to impact thinking and learning and to capitalize on children's innate interest in small things that allow them to control transformations. The portability and intuitiveness of these devices make teachable moments more powerful than ever. With mobile devices that they can manage on their own, when children ask why or how, they can not only get the answers on the spot, but they can also explore deeper with only a few clicks. We've only just begun to explore the potential for early childhood settings. Now you, your staff members, and the families in your program can explore the potential of mobile devices, where the only boundary is the imagination of the person using them.

What are the benefits (from an administrator's perspective)?

- **Affordability:** The cost for a tablet or mobile multi-touch device is typically a fraction of the cost of laptops or desktops, depending on the configuration. You can afford more of them than laptops.

- **Mobility:** The ability to take mobile devices anywhere makes them perfect early childhood companions for teachers and children on the go.

  - **Teachable moments:** Because curious young children thrive on instant interaction to capitalize on their interests and fleeting thoughts, mobile devices let the children explore ideas deeper right on the spot no matter where they are.

  - **Added safety:** It's even more compelling that having smartphones and other mobile devices with teachers on the playground or on field trips can be an additional safety feature, allowing them to be in contact with you, parents, and emergency first responders at all times. Emergency contact information can be stored on the devices, and with a click or two, parents and teachers can be connected. No more lost emergency cards!

  - **Sharing:** Mobile devices are easy to share among classrooms, teachers, and administrators, and with parents.

- **Motivation and "cool factor" for teachers:** There's nothing like novelty to breathe life into programs that have been operating the same way for years. Even the most technophobic and resistant staff members are likely to be at least a little curious, if not captivated, by what mobile devices can do to make their jobs easier and to engage the children in their classrooms.

- **Potential for children with special needs:** Mobile devices possess a stunning capacity to meet the needs of children on the autism spectrum, those with developmental delays, and other disabilities.

- **Potential for parent engagement and narrowing the digital divide:** Because mobile devices tuck nicely into backpacks, the ability to lend technology to families who may otherwise not have has access is huge. Even those who do have access will want to participate in a lending program. This could also be an advantage with multilingual families. Of course, you will need a plan to prevent theft or loss.

- **Can double as a powerful tool for teachers:** Assessment, program monitoring, record keeping, attendance, and other tasks teachers do every day are simplified with iPads and other tablets.

What are the commonsense considerations you need to make about integrating mobile devices into your overall technology plan? Here are the concerns many educators have, and a solution for each:

- **Avoiding loss or theft:** Mobile devices are more prone to being stolen or lost than larger equipment. Fortunately, there are apps that allow them to be traced and located. You can also install theft protection alarms like those used in stores, but that will inhibit the use of the devices on field trips and on the playground. Insuring your equipment is a good idea.

- **Protecting them from damage:** Mobile devices can be fragile. It is easy to find cases to protect them. There are a number of cases designed specifically for preschool children. It is very likely that over the course of the next several years, developers will create more built-in protection. Teaching children how to use technology carefully and intentionally should be among the objectives in your media literacy plan. Backing up the data and apps on these devices is simple and important. The manufactures have made it possible to back up, store, and restore data and applications to the cloud (a server managed and maintained by a vendor), and/or to a local device such as a laptop or desktop computer or your office network. We strongly recommend that you plan accordingly.

- **Planning to avoid distractions for teachers:** Every administrator is likely to worry that the mobile devices could cause teachers to be distracted from the important work of engaging, observing, teaching, and supervising children. Certainly, this is a factor that must be addressed in your role as a supervisor. You will have to develop policies and procedures to manage this potential problem.

- **Protecting confidential information:** If confidential information is stored on the devices, you will need to make sure they are secured with strong passwords, and you may use third-party apps to ensure lockdown. You should limit the number of devices that have information that needs to be secured.

Tips for objectives to include in grant applications:
- Allows children to explore technology and practice skills independently
- Provides easy access to the Internet to expand exposure to information and culture in everyday learning
- Offers individualized activities that meet the unique language and educational needs of each child

- Can be used to engage and involve families in sharing access to technology and in building enhanced literacy practices at home

Special Consideration for Directors: Added Data Costs

The most special aspect of iPads and other tablets is their wireless connectivity. The ability to connect to a Wi-Fi (or wireless Internet) connection and a mobile broadband connection is built into many mobile devices. What's the difference? There is a big difference in terms of ongoing costs, so it is important to know the difference and what it will mean for your bottom line.

In order to have Wi-Fi service, you first have to have Internet access provided by a cable or satellite company or Internet service provider (ISP). Once Internet connectivity is installed, Wi-Fi networks are established by connecting wireless hubs that send signals to hotspots where people can connect their devices to the Internet wirelessly. For example, airports, bookstores, and restaurants frequently offer free Internet access. Customers connect to their wireless networks. The store or restaurants pay for Internet access and allow their customers to use it at no cost. Similarly, you may decide to purchase Internet service for your program and offer it throughout the building to all of the classrooms and common areas. If so, your center (and even the grounds surrounding your center) can be a hotspot, and with permission and passwords, staff and parents or other visitors can log onto your network.

Mobile broadband allows people to connect to the Internet even when they are not in a hotspot. Using an external modem (on a laptop computer) or an internal modem (on mobile devices such as tablets or e-readers), you can even connect in a car, boat, or train, provided that there is service in the area! You must purchase mobile broadband service from the same providers that offer mobile phone service. You cannot use the same plan for two devices, so your phone plan will not cover your tablet or external modem. The plans can be purchased in a variety of packages depending on your expected usage, but if you go over your data limit, you will either be asked to buy move coverage or you will be charged high fees. Most devices allow you to track the usage easily.

Buying mobile broadband and the devices that allow mobile broadband access is clearly optional. As a matter of fact, you may not need it at all. But it is worth considering buying at least one smartphone or mobile broadband tablet or iPad for unexpected emergencies. They come in handy during power outages, field trip emergencies, and other unexpected situations. You can buy relatively inexpensive small data plans that can give you peace of mind for the unexpected.

Comparing Mobile Broadband and Wi-Fi

Feature	Wi-Fi	Mobile Broadband
Must be in a hotspot	Yes	No
Additional fees for "overage"	No	Yes
Can buy in small bundles	No (monthly)	Yes
Can be used on tablets and iPads	Yes	Yes
Can be used on smartphones	Yes	Yes
Can be used on computers	Yes	With an external modem
Purchased service will provide service to multiple devices at once	Yes	No

E-Books and E-Readers

8

Mrs. Bobbi added two e-book readers to the library area of her classroom. Other teachers were skeptical of this untraditional addition, but Mrs. Bobbi had a plan. She realized that she was seeing a changing array of home languages among her four-year-old students—and sometimes new children came in the middle of the year, which gave her little or no time to find books and materials in their languages. Having the e-book readers allowed Mrs. Bobbi to expose all of the children to this new way to use technology and play with electronic books. She was also able to download storybooks in different languages at a moment's notice whenever a new child who spoke a language other than English started in her classroom.

There are many kinds of e-books and many devices with which to read them. However, no matter how far this technology develops, we do not believe we will see the day when there are no more rich, colorful, and inviting book corners in early childhood classrooms. We don't see e-books as a replacement for traditional books, but as an addition to your book collection.

If you are interested in using e-books in your classroom, you may purchase a specific e-book reader, such as Kindle or NOOK Color. If you already have mobile multi-touch tablet devices, however, you don't need an extra piece of equipment because you can use them to store and read e-books.

E-readers use a very small amount of space to store a large selection of books, and they allow you to access books quickly online if you need a book about a particular topic or in a particular language. Because e-readers are not designed to be sturdy enough for young children and they offer few additional features to support learning, you might want to consider purchasing handheld multi-touch devices such as iPod Touch or tablets that contain e-reader capabilities but offer so much more.

For the most part, e-readers supplement paper books. They are not recommended for toddlers because they may not stand up to drooling and biting. You can certainly sit with children and read books from an e-reader as you would paper books, and you would use the same considerations for developmentally appropriate reading activities.

Features of E-Book Readers

Features you may find on e-book readers are as follows:

- Internet access
- Apps with activities to enhance the book experience. For example, one app shows and reads the story of *The Little Engine That Could* and adds music, sound effects, and opportunities for children to select items to fill the train cars.
- Vooks, which are e-books with embedded links that allow readers to dig deeper by going to websites, illustrative videos, or other Internet media
- Blocked or limited sharing
- Bookmarking capability
- Note-taking capability
- Email access (on certain devices)
- Organization that allows you to easily search the books you have
- Capability to collect various translations of a favorite book (on certain devices with certain books)
- Ability to find e-books and download online
- Capability to save a lot of copies in small space
- Ability to load specific books and send e-readers home to encourage family reading activities
- A variety of cost-saving measures, such as online libraries where you pay just a small fee to download a book for a limited time

Keep in mind that once you purchase a book on one e-reader you cannot share it with someone else's device. The device itself would have to be lent out if a family wants to bring home some of your e-books.

411 FOR DIRECTORS AND OTHER ADMINISTRATORS: E-BOOKS AND E-READERS

Considerations

E-readers are similar to iPads and tablet computers, but their functionality is limited and focused on a few simple tasks that replicate those associated with reading. For example, you can "go" to the bookstore (on the Internet), browse and search for books, read sample chapters and excerpts, pay for them, and put them in your (digital) library. You can look through your digital library just as if you were looking at books on a bookshelf. The e-books themselves usually have graphic covers that look like their printed counterparts. You can flip through the (digital) pages with your fingers, highlight sections, make notes, and put in bookmarks. You can also access additional multimedia content and click through to the Internet if the book publisher added those features to the book. There are also thousands of magazines that are available for e-readers.

You can also use e-books on iPads and tablets, so this is where you have to make some decisions about budget and the functionality you need.

	E-book Readers (Kindle, NOOK, and others)	Multi-Touch Tablets (iPad, Galaxy, and others)
Accommodates e-books	X	X
Access to the Internet	Limited	X
Shows digital libraries	X	X
Responds to on-screen touch	NOOK, yes/Kindle, no*	X
Allows use of apps	Very few	X
Access to iTunes store	No	X
Computing applications	No	X
Photo, videos, music	No	X
Price ($–$$$$)	$$	$$$
Internet storage of library	No	Yes
Syncs with other devices	No	Yes

*Some models offer touch-screens; the basic model does not.

Pictures and Videos

9

Mr. José used his digital camera to take a photo of the class garden every day after the seeds were planted. He added the pictures to a growing PowerPoint presentation that he posted for the class to see on the interactive whiteboard, and the children dictated observations about how the plants were changing and what might happen next.

For all the debate about whether to use technology or how much technology to use, there's one piece of technology that has made a significant and uncontroversial contribution to our field. Digital photography and videography have changed the way we think about pictures and how to use them. You can take pictures with expensive digital cameras or cheap disposable cameras, with smartphones, tablets, and other handheld devices. You can purchase tiny, inexpensive video cameras that connect directly to your computer and make the videos available immediately. Some people have thousands of photos on file, and none of them printed out on paper. But digital photography also makes it possible for you to print and copy photos if you want to be able to hold them in your hand.

Digital pictures can easily be shared over the Internet, and with that capacity comes great potential for trouble. Confidentiality, ethics, and the safety of the children, families, and staff must be top priorities. You can use stock photos on your website rather than pictures of people who are actually there. Some programs post photos of classroom activities, field trips, and other activities on their Facebook page, but set the privacy settings so strangers can't view them. It is critical that you get every family to sign permissions for taking and using photos of them and their children while enrolled at your program, and that those permissions are very clearly spelled out.

Short videos of conversations can be captured on your smartphone or multi-touch device. This can be a great way to capture children's language and skill development for portfolio assessments. What might happen if you took a video of what clean-up time looks like when nobody is cooperating, and another video of how it looks when it is going well? Just as videos can be powerful tools for the coaching and mentoring process, they can also be valuable ways to help children gain insight into their own behavior and its consequences. Videos can also be instructive. A video of a successful fire drill this year would help a new child who doesn't speak English to understand this potentially scary event. And sometimes videos are just plain fun.

What you can do with digital cameras? The most important feature of digital cameras is that they allow you to store on a computer any of the still or moving pictures you make, and use them in any number of ways. And that number keeps getting bigger and bigger! Once you take pictures and save them, you can use photo-editing programs to do all kinds of things with them. Many of these programs are so simple you will be able to use them the first time you try. You will be able to sort photos, make collages, cut and crop photos, change colors, rotate and reverse the pictures, even do silly special effects. At the end of this chapter, we will discuss a specific way to use photographs for early learning projects called digital storytelling.

Another great thing about digital pictures is that they can be printed out on any number of media. They can be drastically enlarged on a poster printer. They can be printed on iron-on transfer paper that can be pressed onto almost anything that is flat and made of fabric. There are plain and decorative papers, matte and glossy papers, thick and thin papers. You can print on flexible magnetic sheets to turn photos into magnets; print photos on cardboard to turn them into cards, masks, or puzzles; and print on clear plastic to create a window cling sheet. But don't forget that digital photos should only serve as serious supports for existing high-quality early learning experiences, such as described in the following sections.

Developmentally Appropriate Activities for Preschool/Kindergarten

Children as young as three years old can grasp the concept of taking pictures with a digital camera by squinting into the viewfinder and pressing down the shutter button, and they understand that they can see a tiny version of the picture in the camera but can wait to get a larger version printed out. There are several sturdy digital cameras on the market that are designed for preschoolers to use, and there are many ways to use regular digital cameras as well. Photos can build strong connections between home and school. They can also enhance learning in every domain.

We confidently recommend that every early childhood teacher have a digital camera to use. You will want to achieve a balance between using the photographs for projects you design and create and encouraging independent use of cameras and pictures by the children. Here are some ideas you can try.

Logic and Reasoning: Symbolic representation is a key component of logical thinking and early literacy. Photographs support strong connections between three-dimensional objects and their two-dimensional representations. Young preschoolers can benefit from games that encourage them to match three-dimensional items to their corresponding photographs. As children progress, it's a good idea to challenge them by letting them detect connections between things that don't look exactly alike or are not present. Pictures can also support all kinds of pretend and imaginative play.

Posting photographs of the children in your group engaging in appropriate activities that represent the sections of your daily schedule will make it much easier for children to feel the power of understanding what's going to happen next in their day. In other words, photographic schedules and instructions foster independence because they give children the feeling that they know what's next, and they can get ready for it without waiting for an adult to tell them what to do. Another example is arranging an art activity and setting out photos that show how to use the materials, all without needing to say a word to the children.

Thinking and Learning: Using a camera is not an activity but rather a tool to support other activities. Think of the many ways a child can use a camera to document things he or she is interested in. Let children create their own learning books with photos they have taken and words they choose to describe something that they think is interesting and important. These books can be great topics for discussion—and can also be transferred to the computer for showing on an interactive whiteboard so classmates can join in the discussion.

Math: There are many counting picture books, but consider the value of a class-made book that has counting examples taken from photos of the local community. For example, you could create a book of photos of buildings that children recognize and that show a building with one window, then a building with two windows, and so on. Then, you could print out copies for children to take with them on neighborhood walks so they can identify and talk about the buildings—and then send copies of the books home. Because of their realistic images, photos are also very strong clues in a sequencing activity. They can be used to create and record patterns, comparisons, and quantities. Photographic representations on your various charting and graphing projects can go a long way toward helping children focus on the key items being counted or charted.

Science: Some of the most commonly listed learning objectives for science are learning to observe characteristics, similarities and differences, and steps in a change process. Take pictures of several rocks and sort them by characteristics, or take pictures of some rocks and some mushrooms and talk about how they are alike and different. Take pictures of the same tree every week for a year. Take pictures of the new class pet every week and talk about how it has grown and changed. Take pictures of each step in the cake-making process. Create matching or memory games with photographs of things that float or sink. Use photos to show and document cause and effect, chemical change, growth, and observations. You could read a story about recycling to help the environment. But think about how much more convincing it would be for older preschoolers if you put an old plastic bag out on the grass in the play yard and took pictures of what happened to the grass after a few days, using the images to discuss the damage that can be done when trash is not disposed of properly.

Creative Arts: We should start with the premise that photography is, by itself, a form of art. Earlier in this chapter, we listed many of the ways you can manipulate and print pictures. The first that comes to mind is a collage. You might also think of ways to compile pictures into posters and displays in your classroom that the children help create. Print black-and-white photos, and experiment with different ways to add color and embellishment. Use digital cameras or video to document children's three-dimensional art projects that can't be saved. It is fun to take video of a child creating a work of art because they often talk through it—sometimes even creating a story as they go along.

Language Arts and Literacy: The number one language arts/literacy activity with digital photography? Making your own books! There are several software programs available to make it easy to insert pictures you have, add text, and print out the book in the proper size. But you can make your own book with Word or even PowerPoint slides printed out and bound together. Class-made books allow teachers to create books that reflect the interests, languages, abilities, and needs of the children in the class. Books can be made to document projects or studies in the classroom, field trips, or special events. Photos can be printed on cards and made into literacy-building activities, such as event sequencing or sorting based on a sound or letter.

Pictures serve another important purpose in cognitive development that is linked to literacy development. By capturing events that have already happened, photos help children think and talk beyond the here and now. Pictures provide the opportunity to expand understanding of words and ideas the children are learning today by connecting them with things that happened in other places and times.

Social Studies: Photos of the way the police, firefighters, mail carriers, and other community helpers really look in your neighborhood can make a uniquely relevant book that supports social studies learning. Once you have those photos, you could iron them onto T-shirts to make costumes for dramatic play or acting out stories. You can print them on cardboard and cut them out to make stick puppets or flannel-board pieces. You can glue them on blocks or paper towel rolls to add characters to your block area. In addition to purchased books about the different countries of origin of children in your class, why not add books you've made with the children that contain photos of where they actually came from?

Social and Emotional Development: There's no doubt that photos and video can play a significant role in supporting identity and self-esteem development. Photos can be used to create personalized social stories that you design to help children deal with their own behavior that is causing them problems, or help them navigate difficult social situations. You can purchase cloth dolls with blank faces designed to have a full-face photo of a loved one ironed on; so, for example, a child can hug the doll with his mommy's face when he is struggling with separation. Family scrapbooks of photos can help ease children in their transition into your classroom. Scrapbooks that you compile celebrate each child and how he or she has grown and changed over the year and can ease the children's transition to their next class.

Now, here are two examples—Digital Storytelling and Using Skype and Video Chatting— of how photography and video capabilities can be expanded for extraordinary learning experiences.

Digital Storytelling

A New Jersey kindergarten English-as-a second-language teacher, Monica Schnee, won a national award for her Voicethread digital story. She helped her young multilingual students learn about polar bears, and they all worked together to create a digital story with artwork and words produced by the children. Using the Voicethreads website, they were able to record their own voices reading their own words as the screen showed the illustrations they drew. Once the project was posted, other teachers viewed it and recorded their encouraging comments by voice, typing, or both. The project was made available on the website so families of these ESL students who live in other countries could access the story and contribute their comments as well.

Digital storytelling is a way of capturing still and moving images with words and recorded sound—voice and music—to create and keep a lively, multisensory story. This type of activity is so rich in opportunities for supporting language and literacy development that we find it being used in early childhood classrooms throughout the country. Have you watched a wedding video lately? Many times the video starts with music playing in the background while visually zooming in on still photographs, such as pictures of the spouses' childhood homes and baby pictures, then moves seamlessly to actual video of the ceremony and reception. That is an example of how digital storytelling works.

There are several websites that make that kind of production easy for anyone to learn and use. By providing examples, step-by-step instructions, and user-friendly features, sites such as http://voicethread.com or www.storycenter.org allow you to use your own digital photographs and video clips; record and add voices, music, and sound effects; and create a story. Effects can be added to enhance the drama. You may be able to zoom in or out on pictures, fade in and out, crop, decorate, or highlight.

Other sites such as www.voki.com and http://storybird.com offer a different kind of digital storytelling. You select an avatar—a graphic character that represents you or any character in your story—and provide a voice to that character. There are options for different actions. You can type words and have the characters say them, or you can record your own voice. There are multiple language options as well.

Digital storytelling with these resources has become very popular as an educational tool from preschool through college. There are many blogs, wikis, and other articles that describe new and interesting ways to use this technology for a variety of learning activities that we can hardly imagine. If you want to try this idea, there is more than enough help available.

Using Skype and Video Chatting

Miss Paez was pleased to welcome a new member of her three-year-old class who had just moved to America from Japan. Miss Paez had purchased a number of beautiful books with Japanese stories and artwork, but the little girl did not seem interested in the depictions of the roaring ocean or green mountains. When Miss Paez asked the girl's mom about this, she learned the family had never visited the ocean or mountains, but had lived in a bustling city. The next week, Miss Paez arranged to use Skype to contact the girl's grandmother, who still lived in the family apartment in a high-rise building. The girl's grandmother used her computer camera to show all of the children where her granddaughter had lived before, even bringing the camera out to the balcony so the children could see what the city looked like below. The familiar sights pleased the new girl and gave the other children something to talk about with her as they practiced language together.

Skype is a program that you can download to support video conversations over the desktop, laptop, or some mobile devices, such as an iPad. There are other programs that allow you to engage in conversation while seeing the other person or people or environment, such as www.GoToMeeting.com, video chat on AIM, and video chat on Facebook. They provide a way to use the video-recording capabilities of various devices to support real-time interactions across the Internet. They are easy to use and make communication so accessible that the main obstacle to worldwide connections will just be the differences in time zones. This is another example of technology that is catching on like wildfire in the educational community for all ages and grades. Many teachers are sharing their experiences and ideas in personal learning networks you can access via Twitter (search *edtech*), Facebook, LinkedIn, and Google+, or on teacher forums such as TeacherTube or NAEYC.

Here are some examples for you to try with your early childhood groups:

- Skype with friends and relatives of children to show their previous homes and environments and to practice their home languages.
- Skype with digital pen pals to learn about different lands and cultures.
- Skype with experts for viewing in your classroom. You might not play an instrument, but with Skype you could allow your musically talented brother to lead the children in songs.
- Go on virtual field trips with Skype.
- Use Skype to contact family members during the day. Parents who may not be able to get away from work during the day might be able to have conversations with the children or even read a story to the group and discuss it via the computer without ever having to leave the office.

Other Technology for the Early Childhood Classroom

10

As soon as Mrs. Nelson received a grant to purchase technology for her classroom, she began looking over websites and catalogs. She quickly became overwhelmed by the number of different items that could be considered technology for the early childhood classroom. She wondered how she would sort out which were simply gimmicky toys and which had real, sound, educational value.

As our field moves forward into an increasingly technological world, you will be faced with increasing exposure to advertisements and promotions. While these can be very informative, letting you know about the newest products available, you will want to learn some decision-making skills that will help you distinguish the good from the bad.

First and foremost, look for educational value and then look at other features—as we've shown you in previous chapters—which include versatility, lasting value, and time-tested stability. Even technology experts hesitate to buy a new item when it first hits the market. Rest assured that a little patience can pay off. If a product really is good, chances are it will last, will come out in a new, improved version, and may even have a reduced price as it gets more popular. The following are a few examples of items that have met these criteria for potential success.

Technology Gadgets with Promise for Developmentally Appropriate Practice

Smartpens: Smartpens write on paper, record sound, and have the capability to store the image of what the pen wrote along with whatever sound was happening at the time. You can have recordings of words translated into the languages of the classroom that will be triggered when the pen touches a sticker on a certain label or other item in the classroom. Smart pens can even be set up so that readable stickers are placed in children's books that enable you to play the keywords of the book in the different languages as needed. Teachers can also use these devices to record children's invented spelling, prewriting efforts, and drawings. They are so portable, they can be carried around the classroom and used to read prerecorded information that the teacher or the children can hear in different languages, pronounced correctly. And the teacher can make on-the-spot notes as children are playing and working.

Robotics: Many of us can remember playing with a classic toy from the 1960s called Mr. Machine. He helped us learn to put together gears and make a rudimentary robot. More recently, the study of robotics has grown into a popular extracurricular activity for students who are interested in digital technology, engineering, math, and design. There are several organizations that have developed ways to share robotics with preschool children. One example is a website from Nick Jr., www.nickjr.com/games/widgets-build-a-robot.jhtml. These are activities that preschoolers can understand and explore to better understand what a robot really is and how it works. Preschool, as usual, is a great place to start with this topic. A number of math and science learning goals can be addressed while working on the simplest robot-like creations. Kits are available and websites are devoted to understanding how machines can be made to respond to remote controls and environmental cues, so preschool children can learn the basics while accomplishing their math and science learning, too.

Listening centers: A listening center is a place in the classroom where some type of audio player, such as a CD player or MP3 player, is set up with headphones so children can listen to music and recorded books. Children sit, wear the headphones, which are attached to the listening center, and listen. Listening centers are found in many general education as well as special education classrooms. Listening centers make it possible for you to provide recordings in different languages or for different purposes to meet your educational objectives with particular children. The downside is they really only have one purpose and one use: having children sit and listen passively. With newer types of players that are part of desktops, laptops, or handheld devices, you can spend the same amount of money and gain a great deal of versatility as well as the freedom to move around while learning. For example, with a set of iPods in the classroom, children could be listening to a story about the three little pigs in their home languages while building houses in the block area.

Mini digital voice recorders: With this technology, it is possible to have a very small device—clipped to your belt or in your pocket as you move around the classroom—that enables you to record conversations or other activities that can later be uploaded to your computer. These mini recorders allow you to save recordings to enhance a child's learning portfolio. This technology also enables you to record a child's speech in another language, so you can ask a parent or volunteer later to tell you what that child said and use the notes for the portfolio. If you work with infants and toddlers or children with special needs, these devices will help you to collect accurate records of their babbling and speech attempts to share with parents.

Reading machines: There are small and large versions of this technology—often called card readers—that allow you to print labels with QR codes or bar codes, used to represent spoken words in any language available. A scanner or a scanning app on a handheld device with a camera will let the computer read the coded word aloud. This technology, because it is now more flexible and allows you and the children to actually create QR codes for words you choose to say, can be very helpful in supporting children who are learning a second language or who have a language delay or disability.

Overhead projectors: New electronic overhead projectors, such as LCD projectors, may not be as sophisticated as interactive whiteboard technology, but they are available for less money and can be used to project whatever is on your computer or laptop to a wall, ceiling, or screen. Some multi-touch handheld devices may also be used in conjunction with a projector, and some projectors come with built-in speakers. You can even find machines that can accept input from a JumpDrive and show a presentation that you previously prepared on your own computer. Although this technology does not allow the interactions possible on interactive whiteboards (IWBs), it can be used to show what's on your computer screen, or to show large-sized pages of books or examples of science experiments, and so on.

Technology Gadgets That Are Not Developmentally Appropriate

On the other hand, there are a number of technology gadgets aimed at young children that may not live up to their potential. For the record, it is our opinion that young children should not use an imitation or toy gadget when they are capable of handling real technology. When children are properly engaged, we believe that there is little evidence that having children use imitations is effective in preparing children to use the real thing. That being the case, we recommend caution when considering the following gadgets:

- **Children's "educational computers," which are smaller, less powerful, and often very restricted versions of regular laptop computers or tablets.** Although these computers may have applications and games and are classified as "educational," you, as an educated consumer, need to be the judge of whether you consider those claims to be accurate. This book has provided guidance you can use to evaluate these items and determine whether they are worth using some of your technology budget to purchase.

- **Video game consoles such as Wii or motion-sensing devices such as Kinect for Xbox 360,** as well as some that have been developed specifically for toddlers and preschoolers, offer the advantage of involving gross and fine motor activity. However, we would question whether it is worth the significant expense to purchase these items just for the purpose of getting kids up and dancing, jumping, or jabbing. If there are free ways to get children moving, you might better use your technology budget for more versatile, educationally appropriate purchases.

- **Toy imitations of technology items.** A toy with some buttons to push and things that beep or light up may be fun, but is not likely to get a child any closer to technological literacy. Proponents of developmentally appropriate practice recommend that young children have a variety of toys that stimulate creativity and imagination. Plastic remote controls with googly eyes and silly sounds do not do much to support that goal.

Nine-month-old Wyatt crawls across a field of colorful books, jingling balls, and furry stuffed animals to get to the plain gray remote control. His mom wondered what could be so enticing about this dull object that makes no noises, has no moving parts. Then she realized that Wyatt sees his mommy and daddy holding it quite often, so it must be the most desirable thing in the room!

Early childhood professionals certainly know that one of the most powerful motivators for young children is imitation. It is a key component of early learning. Newborn babies imitate their parents when they smile in response to their parents smiling. A seven-month-old will imitate you when you put on a hat—and have a great laugh about it. A one-year-old will push away her baby food and try to grab your cheeseburger. An 18-month-old will hug and tend to a baby doll—upside down. So, is it a surprise that lap babies try to grab their parents' cell phones? Or that toddlers want to reach up and bang on the computer? These are devices they see their parents using many times a day—devices that effectively capture their parents' attention and make them jump when they make sounds. These devices are part of family life in many homes. So, while we may not be sure that babies **need** experiences with technology, it does seem apparent that they have the same reasons for **wanting** to play with technology.

In our quest to bring developmentally appropriate practices and authentic early learning experiences together with technology, we are not in favor of cartoonish toy imitations of real technology. There doesn't seem to be any evidence that a plastic replica of a cell phone with bright colors, googly eyes, and buttons that play simple songs will have anything to do with a child's ability to understand or use technology. And we find that young children don't seem to need practice with fake devices to learn how to use the real things. If our goal is to expose children in a sensible and educationally sound way to real technology, then we think that real technology is what you should use with them early on, real when you feel it is appropriate to do so.

Special Considerations

11

Special Considerations for Children Under Three

What is the role of technology in early care and education programs for infants and toddlers? This is a seemingly simple question with a multifaceted answer. Some people are in favor of using different technologies quite early, while others prefer not to use any technology at all with the youngest children. There are so many different types of technology and different ways to use them that most people have a view that is somewhere in between. For readers who are interested in bringing some technology experiences into the lives of infants and toddlers, we offer suggestions to help you choose and plan.

For children who are 6–18 months old (preverbal to first words): Perhaps one of the most important contributors to early technology learning will be giving infants and toddlers the chance to see their important adults using and enjoying technology. Starting this early, however, does not seem to give children any advantage in learning or in digital literacy. However, technology is part of our lives, and exploring with it could be just as important as exploring cooking utensils or gardening tools. If you have a computer and you want to engage infants with computer activities, you might show a brief video or story and talk about it in just the same way that you talk about a book with a young child, pointing to pictures and asking questions. Keep in mind that the American Academy of Pediatrics issued a statement in 2011 discouraging the use of passive screen viewing for children under the age of three.

There is also value in just letting the youngest set bang on the keyboard and click a mouse or otherwise touch, feel, and experience computers just as they might a cardboard box, bowl, keys, or spoons. Not much is likely to happen, and we don't advocate making this a regular part of your day with infants and young toddlers, but as they grow, they will become interested in computers because they are a natural part of their environment. There is some software available that is actually designed for this kind of exploration. If the adult buys it, installs it, and types in a password, the program will display an array of activity choices. Once the adult selects one, the program disables the keys and mouse so the baby can bang anywhere on the keyboard to make balloons appear, or cats meow, or blocks topple, and nothing can happen to anything the adults have on their computer until they undo the program.

As of this writing, there are currently few commercially available software applications that are of any value for children from 6 to 18 months, and we suggest caution and good professional judgment when reading marketing claims. Keep in mind that software to protect your computer while infants play with the buttons and touch the mouse and screen may be all that is needed at this age. You may not think of it as educational, but one of the richest experiences you might have with software for infants will be your photo storage and editing programs. One thing that seems to feed baby's brains is having plenty of opportunities to view pictures of faces and of loved ones. Sitting an infant in your lap and showing him or her some photos of his or her parents, siblings, or pets might be a wonderful bonding moment and a chance to use lots of valuable language.

Handheld devices have one feature that makes them perfect for the littlest children—these devices are little, too! But they are vulnerable to drooling, mouthing, and biting, which are nearly inescapable at this age. We do not recommend handing one of these devices over to an infant. With a little one sitting on your lap, however, you will find that handheld devices can add to your interactions with an infant or toddler. You can use the devices to play favorite music, read stories, or talk about photos of family members. Children may learn quite readily to pat and tap the screen to make things happen—even though they might not understand how it works. There are apps designed for the youngest children, but use your judgment to be sure you are not purchasing something that is just a gimmick.

While infants may not be able to take pictures on their own, they most certainly can enjoy them! Having real photographs of familiar items is a keystone of high-quality infant and toddler care. With experience, infants begin to learn that a picture represents a real object—an important component of symbolic reasoning. Pictures of the people a child loves and the environment that is familiar can be shown on a computer or handheld device as the child sits with you. You can expand the learning value of those pictures by using them to create personalized books, blocks, and dolls for each child.

For children who are 18–36 months (verbal toddlers): It is not surprising that children at this stage are able to learn to make things happen on the computer screen by pressing buttons or moving the mouse. Toddlers need guidance to make sense of these experiences. With adult interactions, children may gain from a richer learning experience. For this age, look for activities that are simple and clear—but purposeful. This is just another opportunity for children to spend time exploring with an adult.

Don't select games just because they seem "cute." Think about what the children will learn from the activity you choose, and talk with them about it. Look for programs that provide clear feedback right away as children practice and develop skills. Additionally, software that allows you to manipulate familiar photographs can be fun at this age. Think about ways the computer can enhance the explorations and conversations you have about everyday things, such as looking at pictures of cut fruit on the computer and picking out the fruit that you will actually provide as a snack.

Handheld multi-touch devices are finding their way into the hands of many young children. Some children who are as young as one year, and certainly by 18 months, figure out how to do activities on these devices. At this age, children seem able to use the needed gestures such as swiping, tapping, and selecting icons. They know how to pick games and touch the Back button and so on. There are many apps in the various platforms that have been designed specifically for this age group. The key is to look for apps that offer change, stimulation, learning, and fun, and that have the ability to change with the child.

Some apps targeted for this stage are nothing more than electronic flash cards. However, because the market for these devices is growing quickly, you may be able to find engaging, toddler-perfect activities. For example, look for stories with pictures that have actions, such as touching the tree to make the leaves fall. Some apps, such as the one for the book *The Wheels on the Bus*, allow children to start up the bus and choose whether they want the song sung in English, Spanish, or French or just instrumental. It even allows the child to record her own voice singing the parts of the song. Then, as the song plays, the child can tap and move things on the screen to add actions such as opening and closing the doors and making the wipers go back and forth. There are apps to provide information; apps that present a new twist to classic games, stories, and songs; and apps that allow the child to choose, plan, practice, and draw.

Children between 18 months and three years old are developing language skills that can be supported by using photographs in various forms. Children are most likely to talk about things that are recognizable to them and are interesting parts of their lives. They are particularly fascinated by photos and videos of themselves, so this is a good time to play those up. Keep classroom displays at a height that the children can see, and don't fill the space higher up on the wall. Clutter interferes with young children's ability to attend and focus. It is also important to change things from time to time but not to change everything at the same time. Toddlers can get very attached to familiar things, and you might not realize how upset they will get if certain pictures disappear from the wall.

At this age, pictures can be used as cues, guiding children through schedules, play planning, and desirable behavior. For example, you could respond to a line drawing that reminds you of steps to proper handwashing, but photos of the children engaging in each step would be more recognizable for toddlers.

Next Steps—Special Considerations for Young Children beyond Kindergarten

The world of technology opens wide for children who are six years and older. Their increased cognitive capacity and physical coordination make it possible for them to interact more independently on computers, IWBs, handheld devices, and more. There are many conferences, books, and journals devoted to their burgeoning digital literacy and the educational value they derive from it. We will just provide a few key points to guide you in alignment with the framework we have offered you for preschool technology use.

Some key factors that set 6–8 year olds apart from younger children:

- More older children can read and spell.
- Most have attended at least kindergarten.
- They are out of the preoperational stage of thinking and are into the concrete operational stage.
- They have more developed fine motor skills.
- They are likely to have had some exposure to technology already.

As children enter first grade and beyond, they are likely to be able to read instructions for computer activities, to find the disk or flash drive they need to do the activity they want, to start up the computer, to successfully log on, and to put the flash drive in the computer. They can use the printer, do some basic troubleshooting, and understand the whole process.

If you teach children in first through third grade, you will want to support their expanding capabilities, while keeping in mind the premise of developmentally appropriate practice. Children in these grades can do more learning via abstract representation in computer or Internet activities. The children can exercise their knowledge to learn more and think more. It is best to prepare each child so he or she can use technology in ways that are appropriate for his or her own knowledge and experience. Toward that goal, do a brief technology assessment at the beginning of the school year so you know who has done what and who needs certain kinds of support. This is a great time to plan for buddy learning and watching children progress.

Be sure to teach these children what they need to know—don't assume they know it. Provide plenty of practice and make sure that some of it is based on each child's individual knowledge and behavior.

Parents and Commonsense, Technology-Rich Classrooms

Because you are an early childhood expert, what you say and do has an impact on children *and* parents. Every day, in so many ways, as you work with parents to provide the best for the children in your class, you and the children's parents will learn by observing each other and by communicating with each other about every aspect of their children's early learning experiences, which includes technology use.

Some parents may have extraordinary access to technology at home, and others may have very little. In fact, you may find that your classroom is the first or only place some parents can routinely access technology. If so, you can play an important role in narrowing the digital divide by providing technology access to children who might otherwise have not been able to access materials that their more advantaged peers consider routine. On the other end of the spectrum, you may find that you can turn to some parents for their technology expertise and valuable resources. Regardless of the parents' level of access, you have the opportunity to work with them to craft a vision of what the NAEYC technology position statement deems "the development of healthy media habits."

One of the challenges associated with the new proliferation of amazingly accessible mobile devices is that there are children who see their parents use these devices every day. These devices are slick, shiny, and make cool noises! And parents often give their mobile devices to their children to keep them busy and entertained. You may have been in stores or restaurants or in lines where you have seen parents jabbering with friends or otherwise ignoring their children while their children play with an iPad or smartphone. Or maybe you've seen a parent share a meal with children while the parent uses his or her mobile device and the child clamors for attention and/or the device. In the "old days" we called television the "electronic babysitter." Now there's a name for using digital devices to pacify children: the "Passback Effect," a term for the tendency to pass mobile devices to the back seat of the car to keep children entertained. These are examples of media use that distance adults and children. As an early childhood expert, you can help children and families develop healthy media habits, while making the most of the technology available to them.

One of the most important values you can communicate to families on their journey to healthy media habits is similar to the term *co-viewing*, which is a phrase that suggests that parents and children watch television and videos together. Because this book focuses on interactive technology, not television, we like the term *co-participation*, which means parents and other adults engaging with children when they use interactive technology, rather than passing devices back to children for their entertainment value. As a teacher, you can model, communicate the value of, and provide opportunities for co-participation.

Being a teacher in a technology-rich classroom means intentionally balancing the materials, experiences, and projects you offer every day. You also have the opportunity to be a role model of balance and common sense for children and their parents. In addition to connecting with parents about child development and routine day-to-day issues, you also need to communicate with them about balancing technology experiences with other activities that meet their children's physical, social, emotional, and intellectual needs. You can provide parents with resources and support for healthy media use. And you can involve parents in your classroom technology experiences to provide them with real-life examples of building interactive, personal, and warm connections with their children when they use technology. It is your responsibility, along with the other staff members in your program, to make sure that parents know about appropriate technology use to make a difference for children on both ends of the technology-access continuum. Following are strategies and ideas for building equal access to technology and for providing examples of healthy media use in your technology-rich classroom.

There are many ways in which technology can be a thread in the fabric of your relationship with families, but they fall into three broad categories:

1. Creating opportunities to educate parents about using technology use at home,

2. Planning equal access for individual children and the group, and

3. Using technology to connect and communicate with parents.

Creating Opportunities to Educate Parents

Think of all of the ways you educate parents about their children and your classroom. Let's "technify" a few examples:

- **Open House or "Back to School" Meeting**
  Technify it: Take a digital tour of the classroom. No, we don't mean a PowerPoint presentation. Take your parents around the classroom to introduce the learning centers. As you describe the objectives in the learning center, also explain how technology is used in that area.
  Extension: Videotape key portions of the event and make it available as a podcast so parents can share it with family members who were unable to attend, or they can watch it again to remind themselves of important information shared at the meeting.

- **Interest Area Objective Signs:** Create adult eye-level signs that outline some of the objectives in each learning center so parents (and others) can understand what children learn in each area.
  Technify it: Add a technology objective to each sign.
  Extension: Make the objectives available online—on your program's website or Facebook page. When a child mentions working in the art area that day, the parent can look up the objectives to plan some learning time at home.

- **Classroom or Center-Wide Newsletter**
  Technify it: Add a column about technology use throughout the center to every issue. Include screen shots and photos wherever possible, and always include tips, such as:

- How to set boundaries and limits for technology use, including cautions about dangerous or inappropriate Internet use
- Using appropriate technology tools and activities at appropriate ages
- Using appropriate technology to engage with their children, and avoiding the Passback Effect

Extension: To make the newsletter even more "technified," accessible, and educational, make it an online email newsletter so parents with computer access can view it anytime and anywhere, and those who need to broaden their technology awareness can learn by doing. You can also print out the newsletter and offer it both in print and electronically so you do not exclude families. Offering the newsletter electronically offers unique advantages such as the ability to do the following:

- Link to resources, songs, photos, or videos
- Track who has opened and read the newsletter
- Link to important areas of your website so parents know where to find critical information
- Get the newsletter into the hands of parents no matter where they are and regardless of their schedules

- *Family Photo Books:* Some programs provide materials for parents to make family scrapbooks for children to bring on their first day (and beyond) to ease transitions.

  Technify it: Help parents build their computer skills and connect with their children by inviting them to work with their child using Picasa, PowerPoint, Word, or other programs to create a book about their families, complete with photos. Offer the opportunity and equipment for the parents and children to scan some of their treasured family photos so they can take them home on a flash drive, email them, or store them on a free online photo service. They can print out, email, and otherwise share the book with family members in addition to creating a cubbie keepsake.

  Extension: Send home a question once a month to encourage families to work together to add something to their scrapbook. You might ask them to add a page about something really funny that happened in their family or to describe someone who is not a relative but is very important to their family. Ask them to tell who is and why this person important them.

- *Family Surveys:* Many programs survey parents to find out more about their home lives or to get their input for planning and administering the program.

  Technify it: Add questions about how much access they have to technology and how they use it with and in the presence of their children. If the parents are interested, you can even create a simple home assessment checklist to help parents track their time so they can plan to be more engaged with their children. If you want to add more opportunities to expand parents' technology skills or make the process easier, you can create an online assessment. You can offer parents a choice of how they would like to complete the form.

Extension: If parents seem to respond well to these survey formats, you might use them more frequently to keep them involved in what's happening in their children's day. Use a survey to elicit help as you plan projects or activities. For example, if you are planning to set up a post office project, you might use the survey to ask parents:

1. If they have contacts in other countries who would be willing to exchange letters with the children,

2. If they would like to come in on a Saturday to help build some of the props, and

3. If they have any old greeting cards they could donate for the project.
   Not only does this invite them to participate in the project, but in doing so, it gives them ideas for extending the learning at home.

Planning Equal Access for Individual Children, Families, and the Group

You may wonder how you can begin to level the playing field for families who do not have access to technology. That's a tall order for an early childhood teacher! But with a little creativity and ingenuity, there are small things you can do to allow families to experiment with and enjoy technology with their children. Plan and implement activities that share your equipment in meaningful ways with families. By starting small in the early years and helping families learn about the latest technology along with their children, you can have enormous impact on their future by setting the family on a path to success. Here are just a few examples:

- **"Share the music" backpack kits:** Chances are you include music in your weekly plans. Download the songs onto the classroom MP3 player, iPad, tablet, or other device, and send it home with one child every night. If there is a matching app or music video, add those to the playlist. Add a "co-listening" activity card to the child's backpack that includes instructions about how to operate the device, the lyrics of the songs, activity objectives, and talking points to help parents kick-start their discussions with their children about what they have heard. Be sure these very simple activities and the songs are offered in both English and the families' primary languages.
  Extension: What other technology can you send home? Can you replicate this idea with e-books or other activities? Think outside the box.

- **Create a Parent Access Center:** Do you already have a Parent Area? Work with the administrators and other teachers in your program to add devices and/or stationary computers to the Parent Area. Offer access to the network in your center so parents can scan, print, and access the Internet. Make it available as often as possible, and whenever possible, have the center's technology enthusiasts drop by to help parents use the equipment and software or apps. Better yet, create a volunteer schedule and have other more tech-savvy parents provide support in the Parent Access Center. This is a great way to build connections among parents as well as to offer a service that allows access to technology. If parents are too busy working, try to get community volunteers or interns from local high schools and colleges to help. Short on equipment? Ask for equipment loans or donations for this purpose from local businesses, or try writing a grant for this purpose.

- **Technology Safari:** If you don't have space or equipment for a permanent Parent Access Center, try offering an evening or weekend event in which parents can come to the center to explore the various equipment, devices, and applications you have throughout your center. You will want to plan for rotation through specific projects or activities at stations, such as a moving safari, so parents and family visitors know what to do. Otherwise, they might very well look at the equipment and smile but do nothing. Assign children to be "Technology Safari Guides" to help with specific activities.

Using Technology to Connect and Communicate with Parents

If technology access were equal for all families, building connections and networks with and for parents would be easy. One thing we do know is the digital divide is oddly narrower when it comes to membership in social media sites and the use of texting. We find that families who have no other access to technology may still have a phone with data service or a smartphone, and even if their smartphone is their only access to the Internet, they are likely to participate in Facebook, LinkedIn, or Twitter.

Using technology to connect with and on behalf of parents means much more than pushing out information to them. The point should be to get parents to engage with you online. This should be a two-way communication between you and the parents, and multi-way communication among the parents. This is just another way to build communities, especially for parents who are very busy and unable to make it to the center often.

Here are a just a few examples of ways you can use technology to connect with parents and build networks for them:

- **Text Messaging**
  - Text parents (with their permission, of course) a learning-extension idea each day. For example, you might text: "We talked about beans today. Ask your child what his or her favorite legume is," or "We read *Brown Bear, Brown Bear* today. How many pictures of animals can you and your child find in your house?"
  - Text links to articles and blog posts, or even information on the center's website.
  - Send photos of children engaging in activities at school during the day.
  - Make yourself available by text messaging during breaks and specific hours during the evening so parents can connect with you as needed.

- **Email**
  - Email newsletters and announcements to keep parents informed.
  - Encourage parents to communicate with you and each other by email as well. Ask for permission to share an online classroom or center directory that includes email addresses and cell phone numbers. Parents should have the ability to control whatever information you publish about them, including the option to opt out of the directory altogether.
  - Email photos of children engaged in fun and learning during the day. (This is especially helpful when parents don't speak much English.) Invite parents to share photographs with you by email, too. Use the photos to decorate the room, cubbies, or in a surprise online gallery or presentation to share with the entire class.

- **Website and Online Services**
  - Use your center's website to create a classroom or center blog where you post interesting activities in which teachers have tried using technology with the children. For example, "Big ideas from Miss Suzy's class today—The children took digital photographs of ice cubes melting on the playground at different times of the day. The children created a class presentation on the whiteboard explaining how the ice in the sun melted faster than the ice in the shade." Blogs are supposed to be interactive, so invite parents to respond with their questions and ideas. You want parents to engage with you on the blog, unlike the rest of the website, which is probably less interactive.
  - Use some of the commercially available programs to create portfolios to share each child's progress with his or her parent. Many programs allow you to scan drawings and upload other digital content that documents children's

progress, as well as allowing for observations. Some offer very sophisticated assessment systems. Of course, you can simplify the portfolio idea by creating your own version in Word, PowerPoint, or other software.

- Set up a Facebook page for your center or classroom. Use it to inform parents about classroom activities; to share online resources, photos, videos, and links; and most of all, to start conversations with parents. Facebook is a place to interact, not just pass on information. This is also a place where parents will connect with one another, so offer exchanges of information that encourage parents to interact with one another.

- Use free online survey tools to ask parents for their input on a regular basis. You can even send links to the surveys by text message, email, or on your Facebook page.

Use all of the techniques above to connect parents to community resources such as the local child care resource and referral agency, community health services, local schools, disability agencies, job training and placement agencies, continuing education, and other resources. Providing links to these services makes the connections much more immediate than handing them a phone number.

Hopefully, these ideas will inspire you to work with parents and make them an important part of your program's technology plan. Together, you and the children's parents can provide a great start in the education of their children toward a bright future.

Digital Literacy for Teachers and Children

13

As a teacher, you know *literacy* means being able to decode and understand language and to use language. You understand the profound impact literacy has on almost every aspect of life in every country around the world. You may not have considered the importance of *digital literacy*—the ability to find and use information and to communicate using digital technology. As we discussed in Chapter 1, there is still a lot of controversy about how important it is to include technology and digital literacy in early childhood classrooms. But, there is no denying the fact that as a teacher today, you may need some basic digital literacy skills just to function in your job. No matter what you decide about including technology in your classroom, you

may have to use it to accomplish some of the other tasks related to your work. Ultimately, if you decide to integrate technology into your classroom experiences, you will also have to help the children in your class with their digital literacy.

Teaching "Digital Natives"—and Leveling the Playing Field

There's some good news about planning to provide digital literacy experiences in your classroom: Depending on the backgrounds of the children in your classroom, it actually may be relatively easy to teach them digital literacy. Even if the children have varying degrees of exposure to technology, they are already "digital natives," or people who were born into a digital world and know no other way of life. You know it is easier to teach in one language than it is to teach a second language. It is the same for digital literacy. Digital natives will intuitively absorb the skills they need because they already speak the language. In fact, depending on your age or background, it might be easier to help children use technology tools than it will be for you to learn what you need to know yourself!

But do not be lulled into thinking all children are techno-ready. There is a serious and profound digital divide between children who live in poverty and those who come from families with more resources. Obviously, the children with fewer advantages may also have fewer opportunities to use technology. However, these days it is almost impossible to have not been exposed to *some* technology. It is more a matter of how much hands-on experience children may or may not have had. If you decide to introduce technology into your classroom, you have the possibility of leveling the playing field by providing opportunities to all children, and perhaps even their families. This book provides a few ideas and tips about how to get started doing your part to erase the digital divide in your classroom.

What about you? Are you a digital native, or are you trying to learn "technobabble" as a second language? Before you can integrate technology in your classroom, you must be digitally literate enough to be comfortable working with the basic tools. In this chapter we're going to help you learn more about what you need to know. Chapter 15 offers directors and other administrators guidance about how to offer the training and support you will need.

What Is Digital Literacy?

There are many ways to look at the types of literacy skills adults and children need today and will need in the future. The NAEYC position statement on technology (available at www.naeyc.org) outlines the importance of *digital literacy,* which we define as the ability to find and use information and to communicate using digital technology. The chart that follows clarifies how we will describe the difference between digital literacy and media literacy, and the many skills we all need to be digital citizens and informed media consumers.

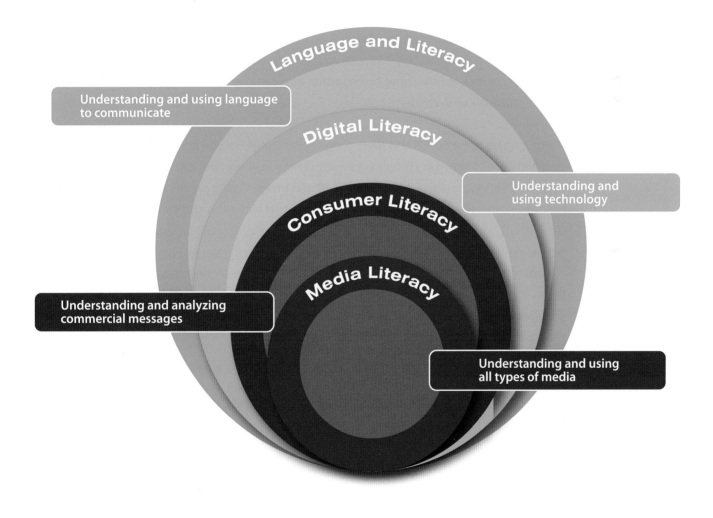

We're going to zoom in on and take a quick look at digital literacy for teachers and children in early childhood settings. This is a pretty big topic that spans everything from basic computer skills to online security and privacy and everything in between. As a matter of fact, digital literacy for early childhood deserves a book all its own! Because we can't cover everything, we'll focus on what we believe are the top five priorities for teachers and children:

1. Basic hardware and software skills
2. Internet skills
3. Online safety, security, and privacy
4. Media literacy: communication and locating and analyzing credible information online
5. Online consumer awareness

We will take a look at how these five priorities apply to you personally and professionally and to your work with children.

Wait! Don't be turned off! If this topic conjures up images of you and/or the children in your class sitting down at computers for lessons on keyboarding and other computer skills, wipe those images away! Replace them with the images you have of how adults and children learn best—with hands-on exploration, trial and error, and some commonsense facilitation by a supportive teacher or mentor. Of course, you will have to be intentional to weave digital technology into your life and into your classroom. You may need to take a class or find ways to learn a few basics as well as support the children as they learn. Just like everything else you learn yourself and all of the other content you address in your program every day, you will have to plan to ensure you and the children in your class learn the basics.

First, All about You, the Teacher in a Digital World!

Obviously, if you plan to evaluate technology, you need to know a little about technology tools yourself. Start by assessing what you know and what you need to learn. Here's a simple checklist to help you get started.

Digital Literacy Skills Self-Assessment Chart

I. Hardware and Software Skills	Got It	Need to Learn
I can log on, log off, open, use, and close programs.		
I understand and use the functions of the mouse and/or touch pad.		
I know what an icon is and what to do with it.		
I know how to drag icons and files.		
I know how to open up multiple programs at a time and how to move quickly between them.		
I know how to use the on-screen help offered in most programs and applications.		
I know how to download and install programs.		
I know how to search for a file on my computer.		
I know how to create a folder.		
I know how to store files on external media including USB drives, CDs or DVDs, or external hard drives.		
I know how to create secure passwords and how to change them often to protect privacy.		
I know how to access and download photos and videos from cameras. I know how to download audio files from MP3 players and Apple devices.		
I know how to add new hardware such as scanners, mice, keyboards, printers, and other devices.		
I know how to use the basic functions of a touch screen.		
I know how to use the basic functions of a mobile device or smartphone, including loading and using apps.		
I know what a font is and how to change fonts in documents.		
I know how to modify margins, tabs, headers, footers, page numbers, and line spacing in my word-processing software.		

I. Hardware and Software Skills (continued)	Got It	Need to Learn
I know how to edit, copy, cut, and paste a block of text in my word-processing software.		
I know how to create a table in a word-processing document or presentation.		
I can use the spell-checker tool in my word-processing software.		
I know how to insert graphics and other files into a document or presentation.		
I know how to save a document, presentation, or spreadsheet and use Save As to change the format or saved location of the document.		
I know how to create a simple spreadsheet with rows, columns, and headings in spreadsheet software.		
I know how to create a simple presentation complete with photos and other graphics using presentation software .		

II. Internet Skills	Got It	Need to Learn
I know how to connect to the Internet.		
I know how to go directly to a website using the site URL address.		
I know how to search for a website using a search engine like Google or Yahoo.		
I know how to save, print, or forward a webpage.		
I know how to bookmark webpages so I can go back to them later.		
I know how to download, decompress, and open documents and programs (for example, applications, presentation files, or PDF files).		
I know how to log on and log off of password-protected websites.		
I know how to construct a search for an exact phrase.		

III. Online Safety, Security, and Privacy	Got It	Need to Learn
I know how to use and maintain up-to-date antivirus and security software programs, and I use them regularly.		
I know at least three ways to avoid having my computer become infected with a virus.		
I know how to manage my computer password and the passwords for the various systems I need to use.		
I know how to avoid email and online scams.		
I never share my password, username, Social Security number, credit card, banking information, or other sensitive information online unless I am confident the site is secure.		
I know what *https://* means before the www in a website URL.		
I know how to adjust my security settings on social media sites.		

IV. Media Literacy: Communication and Locating and Using Credible Information Online	Got It	Need to Learn
I have a personal email address and know how to use it.		
I have a work-related email address and know how to use it.		
I know what a listserv or electronic discussion group is.		
I know how to attend a webinar.		
I know how to manage and attend online classes.		
I know how to participate in online chats.		
I use social media sites like Facebook, LinkedIn, and Twitter, and I know how to stay safe on these sites.		
I understand the difference between blogs and websites.		
I know how to find credible information on the Internet.		
I know how to evaluate the credibility of a website or the information on the website based on the authority of the website owner, its accuracy, and objectivity.		

IV. Media Literacy: Communication and Locating and Using Credible Information Online (continued)	Got It	Need to Learn
I know that all images, words, and sounds, except information explicitly said to be "in the public domain" or tagged with a Creative Commons registration mark, may be copyrighted, and use of these original expressions may require permission of the copyright holder.		
I know how to determine the source of a website.		
I know how to critically evaluate the information I read online based on the source.		

V. Online Consumer Awareness	Got It	Need to Learn
I can discern between paid advertisements and other information on websites, social networks, and search engines.		
I understand that when I fill out forms online, I may be "opting in" to receive email from companies.		
I know how to avoid in-app purchases I do not intend to make.		
I know how to determine if a website is safe and secure for online purchases.		
I know how to locate contact information for the companies with which I do business online.		

Pay It Forward! Getting the Background You Need to Work Effectively with Young Children

If you've just completed the Digital Literacy Skills Self-Assessment Chart, you now have an idea of your skills, your strengths, and the areas in which you need to pursue more knowledge. Once you have those skills, you will be ready to share them with the children in your classroom. Of course, learning all of the basics may mean that you need to get some formal training, or maybe all you need is to sit down with someone else who has more technical skills and abilities. Perhaps you need a combination of hands-on practice and an encouraging mentor. You might add some of these professional development needs to your annual performance evaluation, and ask your supervisor for support along the way. Remember, Chapter 15 offers ideas for administrators who plan to support staff members with their technology professional development plans, so you may want to share this book with your supervisor.

So, let's say you have some basic skills and you want to integrate technology in your classroom. How do you make sure that the children have the background they need to make use of the tools you integrate into your classroom? Of course, it will depend on what tools you plan to use, but remember, our young digital natives, depending on their home experiences, may be savvier than you think. You will probably spend more time helping them with more of the media-literacy, safety and security, and consumer-awareness skills than the actual use of the hardware and software. They will learn most of what they need to through experience, modeling, and your encouragement.

You will still need to be intentional about technology use because simply placing technology into your classroom is not likely to help you achieve your objectives with children. Plan experiences that help children learn to:
- Be intentional when they use technology.
- Limit the time they spend using technology.
- Navigate the Internet safely.
- Identify and avoid scams and enticing marketing.
- Use the Golden Rule, and treat others as you would like to be treated online
- Defend themselves against cyber bullying.

You Are the Gatekeeper for the Children in Your Program: Sorting Out the Information You Encounter

One of the most important skills you will need is the ability to sift through and sort out the information you encounter on the Internet. It is especially important to be a critical consumer of information when you select sites to use with the children in your class. You are the gatekeeper to their access to the Internet, and it is a big responsibility. As a precaution, children should not be able to access the Internet in your classroom without your support, and you should always have an adult nearby when children are using devices. You should also buy, download, and install internet filtering software and/or apps (that you can find with a quick Internet search) on the devices in your classroom, in order to limit unacceptable exposure to inappropriate content. It seems like it would be easy to find developmentally appropriate interactive sites for young children, but it can be confusing. Remember, open-ended interactivity with meaning and purpose are the core of what you want in websites for children.

You are the gatekeeper to their access to the Internet, and it is a big responsibility.

Some people think that one way to evaluate the quality of the site is to determine what type of organization runs the site. For example, web addresses that end in *.org* are operated by nonprofit organizations. Websites that end in *.com* are often owned by companies. It seems logical that nonprofit sites might offer higher-quality content. While many of the .org websites are excellent, sites with .org extensions do not necessarily offer appropriate content. Conversely, there are some fabulous, highly interactive, and appropriate sites for children that are operated by for-profit companies. Regardless of the profit status of the organization offering the site, you must evaluate the appropriateness of the site before you allow children to have access to it.

It is true that some websites use misleading tactics to make money, and the children in your program should be protected from these tactics. If you are visiting a .com site, one aspect to consider is why the company offers the service—how does it make money? Does the site lure visitors to click to make purchases? Does it lead to inappropriate content? All kinds of websites may or may not have hidden agendas, but you have to be a critical thinker and computer user to make that decision. It will be your job as gatekeeper to make some of these decisions for the children, and it will also be your responsibility to teach them how to be critical decision makers, too. Your digital literacy teaching should include helping children learn to recognize credible websites and to spot and avoid advertisements and suggested purchases. Planning learning experiences around these concepts is a good way to help children exercise critical thinking skills and is part of the digital literacy learning process.

A good rule of thumb is to rely on companies you already know and trust for great materials for children. For example, the Public Broadcasting Service (PBS) offers high-quality interactive content for young children, parents, and teachers. Sesame Workshop and the National Geographic "Little Kids" site also offer appropriate content for young children. However, Nickelodeon, which is well known for children's television content, is a site you might want to carefully explore and evaluate before you proceed with the children, because the Nick Jr. website includes very intrusive advertising. Some of the games and experiences on this site are appropriate, but some are simply entertaining, rather than beneficial. For more information about good sites for children, consult www.LittleClickers.com, an excellent resource for teachers looking for good content for young children. Little Clickers is also a monthly column in *Children's Technology Review,* a highly trusted journal that focuses on all kinds of digital applications for children of all ages. Common Sense Media is also a trusted resource of information for reviews of all kinds of children's media, including websites. Finally, use the chart on page 59 to evaluate the sites to which you allow access.

Part of your job will be to help children learn to apply the same critical thinking skills that you use to make good choices online. Yes, you will be the gatekeeper when children are in your classroom, but the ultimate goal is to help them form healthy media habits early.

Helping Children Navigate the Internet Safely

Before we talk about what children need to know to protect themselves online, as the gatekeeper to the Internet, you need to install and know how to use antivirus, security, spam (unsolicited email)-filtering, and Internet-safety software, and how to adjust the settings on the computers in your classroom to protect the children. There's a lot to know. We suggest you work together with your supervisor or director to coordinate this effort for the entire organization.

Because the children you teach are so young and are preliterate, you will do most of the work to protect the children when they are online. If you are not working with them, station an adult near the equipment, and restrict access to only the sites you allow. Just as we teach children how to avoid "stranger dangers" and protect themselves in real life, we have to help them protect themselves online. There is an amazing array of fantastic resources to help you offer experiences to help children learn to protect themselves online. Common Sense Media (www.commonsensemedia.org) is a great resource for more information, as is (believe it or not) the Federal Bureau of Investigation site, which offers useful advice at www.fbi.gov/stats-services/publications/parent-guide and at www.fbi.gov/fun-games/kids/kids-safety. The National Center for Missing and Exploited Children also offers great resources on its NetSmartz site (www.netsmartz.org/Parents).

Here are seven Internet-safety tips for children, adapted from suggestions in "Internet Safety Tips: Grades K-3" by www.WebWiseKids.org.

1. **Have an adult nearby.**

   Always get permission from an adult to use the computer or device. Make sure an adult knows what you are doing and is nearby in case you need help.

2. **Protect your computer.**

   Keep food and drinks away from the equipment, and handle it gently. Ask for help to attach other devices or download software. Do not download software without an adult's help. Do not click on links in emails or unknown websites. Only go to sites an adult has approved.

3. **Protect your privacy.**

   Keep your passwords, name, address, phone number, hometown, school name, or other information about you or your family private. Use a fake nickname when using sites that ask for your name. Say no to strangers online, and tell an adult if anything unusual happens on the computer when you are using it.

4. **Protect the privacy of others.**

   Keep information about your family, friends, school, and teachers secret.

5. **Beware of contests, prizes, sign-up forms, and gifts.**

   Always ask an adult for help if you see a form you need to fill out. When someone offers a prize or gift, he or she might want to get you to share private information.

6. **Beware of strangers. Say no to messages.**

   Say no to strangers online. You would not walk away with a stranger if you met one in person. The same is true online. The person may pretend to be a friend or a child or a family member, but because you cannot see the person, you cannot be sure. Do not chat with strangers online. Get an adult if you get a message from a stranger.

7. **Use the Golden Rule online.**

   Treat people the way you would like to be treated, but remember, it's okay to say no and close down the activity if you get a message from someone you don't know or if someone is bullying you. Then ask an adult for help right away.

Professional Development: Taming Technology

14

It's time to take a look at your personal objectives for integrating technology in your classroom, to evaluate the skills you have, and to identify the skills you need to develop in order to achieve your goals. So let's take a look at where you are now, where you are going, and what you need to get there. The following self-assessment questionnaire is a simple way to figure out what the next steps are.

Basic Computer and Technology Operations and Concepts

Check the boxes to assess your level of proficiency, whether your use of the technology tool is for personal or professional use or both, and whether the tool is a priority for your class or not. Review the results to discover the areas in which you have no or little experience, and use the information to plan your professional development objectives.

Technology Self-Assessment Form

	Tool	Level of Proficiency				Personal/ Professional Use		Priority Y/N
		Not Yet	Emerging	Capable	Expert	Personal	Professional	
Hardware and Devices	Desktop computer							
	Laptop computer							
	iPad or tablet							
	Digital still camera							
	Digital video camera							
	Scanner							
	Printer							
	Smartphone							
	MP3 Player or iPod							
	Interactive whiteboard (IWB)							
	Multi-touch table							
	Talking pen/Smartpen							
	E-book reader							
	Other							
Desktop, Cloud Computing Software, Apps	Operating systems (PC/MAC)							
	Word processing							
	Spreadsheets							
	Presentation							
	Photo editing							
	Databases							
	Child Management							
	Child and program assessment							

	Tool	Level of Proficiency				Personal/ Professional Use		Priority Y/N
		Not Yet	Emerging	Capable	Expert	Personal	Professional	
Desktop, Cloud Computing Software, Apps (continued)	Browsers (Firefox, Internet Explorer, Safari)							
	Acrobat							
	Chat							
	Video chat							
	Blog management							
	Facebook							
	Twitter							
	YouTube							
	Other social media sites							
	Website management							
	Survey systems							
	E-learning							
	Webinars							
	Podcasts							
	E-learning platforms							
	Other							
Communi-cations	Internet browsing and searching							
	Basic wireless (Wi-Fi) access							
	Syncing mobile devices							
	Bluetooth devices							
	Smartphone							
	Texting							
	Other							

	Tool	Level of Proficiency				Personal/ Professional Use		Priority Y/N
		Not Yet	Emerging	Capable	Expert	Personal	Professional	
Educational Technology (Techniques and tools you use in your classroom)	Technology in ECE settings							
	Software specific :_____							
	Software specific :_____							
	Software specific :_____							
	Hardware specific :_____							
	Hardware specific :_____							
	Hardware specific :_____							

Professional Development, Coaching, and Mentoring

Now that you have assessed your level of proficiency with common technology tools, take a look at the areas in which you need to learn more and the areas in which you excel. Determine if the areas in which you lack understanding or ability are important for what you hope to achieve with technology in your classroom. If you want to use those specific technology tools in your classroom but need to learn more, you will need to seek resources and training in formal courses, and you should also look for mentors within your program, among your family and friends, or in your center or school community. In the areas in which you are capable or expert, consider offering your support as a mentor and coach to staff members or other center community members. Because we know professional development and learning are lifelong processes that require much more than classroom training, coaching and mentoring—whether you are receiving or offering—are important parts of your technology plan. Think about seeking support from those who know more and offering support to others who know less.

Obviously, when planning your technology-related professional development, you will need the support of your supervisor. This book includes a section designed to help supervisors understand their role in supporting teachers in technology-rich programs. (See Chapter 15, Building and Supporting Commonsense, Technology-Rich Programs.) If your supervisor has not already read this book, the information and guidance in that chapter could be a valuable way to begin a conversation about what you need for your classroom.

If you participate in annual or semi-annual performance evaluations, you may want to consider adding some professional development objectives and goals to your formal self-assessment. Performance evaluations are the right time to ask for additional training. If your program does not have a formal performance evaluation process, prepare a brief technology professional development proposal and give it to your supervisor. Include some goals and objectives for technology in your proposal, and describe how those objectives will help the children in your classroom, their parents, and other staff in the organization. You may want to include your Technology Self-Assessment Form. Just remember that your supervisor might have other plans for your professional development, so be prepared to discuss your options after hearing your supervisor's plans.

Finding the Right Professional Development

There are a variety of options for training and ongoing technical assistance for technology professional development. First, you may have to learn some skills. Depending on what you want to do and how much knowledge you already have, the course level can vary from basic to advanced. For example, you may already know a bit about using the center's new iPads, but you need to know more to be able to use them to create photo galleries for the classroom. You might be able find training on using iPads for this purpose at your local Apple store or online, or you might find other resources.

Training classes are just the tip of the iceberg. We know that children and adults learn best when:

1. The activities are personally relevant and meaningful,
2. The learners can apply what they have learned on the spot,
3. There are ample opportunities to apply and practice the skills and concepts in real-life situations, and
4. The learners are supported with encouragement and positive models.

Training classes and courses offer great hands-on opportunities to learn, but they typically do not offer ongoing support through coaching and mentoring. Depending on the length of the course and how frequently it is offered, the course may not offer the ongoing practice needed to develop the skills you need or provide the opportunity to apply the skills and concepts in real life through meaningful and relevant situations. Therefore, courses and workshops are best for teaching foundational skills. Using the technology tools in a supportive environment with coaching will be more effective for building core technology competencies in the long term. In other words, your technology professional development plan should include a variety of methods of learning.

Let's take a look at the basics first.

The Basics: Skill and Concept Development Training (Even If It Is at an Advanced Level)

1. **Part- or full-day hands-on computer lab training offered by individual consultants, companies, device and software manufacturers, or computer training organizations**

   Advantages
   - Lab training is great for practical skill development about specific processes, software, or applications.
   - Short bursts of training can be very valuable for learning very specific skills and when time is limited.
   - This is also an excellent approach for people who are already fairly skilled in a specific skill or with specific tools, but want to advance to the next level or prepare themselves to train others.

   Disadvantages
   - The shorter duration might not be enough to ground the skill or concepts so they can be used in practical situations.
   - The activities in the session may not be practical or relevant. Using "practice" data or scenarios that are out of context often leave the learner perplexed.
   - This format may not offer enough time to practice and apply the skills.
   - This training doesn't offer time for reflection, discussion, and assessment.

Caution: Make sure that the credentials of the organization that provides the training are reputable and the trainers are experts. Try to get recommendations from other people who have participated in training provided by the organization or with the trainer.

2. **Multiweek, hands-on lab training offered by individual consultants, private companies, or computer-training organizations**

   Advantages
   - Better than "one-off" or single training sessions because skills are broken down into manageable segments and can be practiced in your classroom, center, or home between sessions over a period of time.
   - Good for learning more complex technology concepts or tools

   Disadvantages
   - While better than single "one-off" training seminars, for less-experienced users and very complex solutions, this approach may not be enough to build sustainable skills.
   - This approach may not offer time for reflection, discussion, and assessment.

3. **Semester-length, "for-credit" courses offered through colleges, universities, or computer training organizations**

   Advantages
   - Best for duration and interval application of skills and concepts
   - Typically offer time for reflection, discussion, and assessment

   Disadvantages
   - The courses can be costly.
   - The courses are time consuming.

4. **Long-duration courses offered by nonprofit organizations for educators or other nonprofit organizations**

   Advantages
   - The courses may be less costly than other courses.
   - It's helpful to have courses designed and led by people who are focused on education.
   - The courses are best for duration and interval application of the skills and concepts.
   - The courses typically offer time for reflection, discussion, and assessment.

   Disadvantages
   - The courses are time consuming.

5. **Software, hardware, or device-specific training offered by the manufacturers**

   Advantages
   - The training is usually less costly, and often free.
   - Training is often offered onsite.
   - The training is often offered before the software or device is installed.
   - This training is taught by expert users of the specific tool who are familiar with your organization and how the tool is used in your setting.

   Disadvantages
   - This training may only be offered at the time of the purchase and not when new staff members are hired.
   - Trainers may not understand early childhood education. (Some do.)
   - The training is very specific to one tool.

6. **Online live training offered as a single webinar or a series of webinars**

   (Sometimes called synchronous e-learning, webinars are live sessions with an instructor who provides instruction over the Internet. Participants watch and sometimes participate in a demonstration, using their computer screens to see the visuals and using phones or computer speakers to hear the audio components.)

   Advantages
   - This training is taken at work or home from a computer. It is not necessary to travel to another location, and it occurs at a specific time of day.
   - This training is often less expensive than live training.

- Short bursts of training can be very valuable for learning very specific skills and when time is limited.
- Good for people who are already fairly adept at a specific skill or with specific tools but want to advance to the next level

Disadvantages

- This approach requires some understanding of computers to participate.
- This approach requires a fair amount of self-motivation to stay on task.
- This may be just demonstrations of the tool, which are less effective than hands-on practice. (Some webinar presenters do offer opportunities for participants to control the application. Check with the provider to be sure.)
- The shorter duration might not be enough to ground the skill or concepts so they can be used in practical situations.
- The demonstration in the session may not be practical or relevant. Using "practice" data or scenarios that are out of context may be confusing.
- This approach frequently does not offer time to practice and apply the skills.
- This approach does not offer time for reflection, discussion, and assessment.

7. **Online self-paced courses, often called *asynchronous e-learning* (**Most self-paced courses are taken whenever the learners want to take them, as long as they are completed in a specific period of time. The participants log in to a website where the assignments, simulations, videos, and other materials are posted. Learners follow the instructions and respond by taking online tests or posting written assignments for review by the instructor. Many colleges and universities, private institutions, and organizations offer self-paced e-learning courses.)

Advantages

- Courses are taken right at work or home from a computer at any time of day or night. Travel is not necessary.
- Courses are sometimes less expensive than live training.
- Short bursts of training can be very valuable for learning very specific skills and when time is limited.
- Good for people who are already fairly adept at a specific skill or with specific tools but want to advance to the next level
- The longer duration and intervals allow people to apply the skills and concepts between sessions.
- Courses typically offer time for reflection, online discussions, and assessment.

Disadvantages

- This approach requires some understanding of computers to participate.
- Courses only offer hands-on application of skills between sessions, not with the instructor, which makes it difficult to ask questions on the spot.
- This approach requires highly motivated, interested, and engaged learners to sustain interest.

- This is not a great approach for beginners or people not familiar with the Internet.

8. **Professional learning networks (PLNs)** (Professional learning networks are groups of people with similar interests in learning about specific topics. Traditionally, PLNs met in person. Now, the Internet has made it possible to connect people with the same interests or learning objectives through forums, social networking sites, and other groups that may or may not be related through a professional association, school district, or other institution. While many of the groups may not offer formal training, they do offer invaluable resources, ideas, and support.)

There are hundreds of online platforms that can be used as PLNs. Facebook, Twitter, LinkedIn, Ning, email discussion groups, forums on association websites, and other interactive sites allow teachers and administrators to share ideas and resources, ask questions, and discuss issues with one another. A quick Internet search or a search on any of the specific sites on a specific topic will lead teachers to communities of other early childhood educators who are ready, willing, and able to share their wisdom.

Advantages

- Online PLNs are available 24 hours a day, 7 days a week, and 365 days a year from anywhere in the world, making them convenient and highly accessible.
- Building strong bonds with other teachers in online networks often provides a source of strength.
- Online PLNs bring together opinions and ideas from far-flung locations that can provide new cultural insights and perspectives that might otherwise never be accessible to those who can't travel to conferences or other venues.

Disadvantages

- Having discussions with people in writing can't really replace conversations that take place in person.
- It is easy to misinterpret the intentions of others when you can't see their expressions and body language. Misunderstandings are common.
- Interpreting languages can be more difficult in writing.

Regardless of the level or intensity involved in the type of professional development you select, you still can apply what you have learned through your training using the tools that are available to you. You will need to take responsibility for immediate and regular practice by using what you have learned. If you don't touch the technology for a week or two, you may lose most of what you learned. This means you will need to use technology in your classroom as well as seek outside resources.

Beyond the Basics: Using Technology to Learn about Technology

Once you have some basic skills and understanding of technology, you can use that knowledge base to build on your skill level, learn what you need to know about technology, improve your technology knowledge and skills, and get support when you need it. You may find it helpful to join networks of people who share your passion and interests and can provide additional information and support. You can build live networks in your school community and the broader community, and online social networking sites also offer great opportunities to connect with professional learning networks that are already there and waiting for you to join.

While nothing can really replace supportive supervisors and experienced colleagues as resources, with the Internet, the world is your oyster! There are thousands of your peers and colleagues on Twitter, Facebook, and LinkedIn, and on email discussion groups and online forums. The participants in these groups offer a wealth of amazing resources from around the world 24 hours a day, 365 days a year. Like-minded people who are not necessarily part of your network or professional organization join these online professional learning networks and post problems, ideas, resources, and questions—and others post responses. Joining these groups will suddenly open doors with resources you never may have found elsewhere. All you have to do is search for *early childhood, preschool, child care,* or other relevant terms in your favorite social media site or a search engine, such as Google. Among the results you receive, you will find a world of online communities of others sharing ideas and resources. You will be amazed at the resources at your fingertips.

You can also use technology to learn more about technology. When experienced technology users have a problem, idea, or question, the first thing they do is type their question right into a search engine to find the answers. When they search, they find thousands of potential solutions and answers. Using a search engine to find answers to questions, especially about technology-related problems or questions, is a great way to get instant answers. By just typing in the problem you are experiencing or asking for a definition, you will find that the results can not only help you develop confidence in your own troubleshooting abilities, but also solve problems quickly and independently without waiting for experts to help you.

YouTube offers a wealth of instructive videos on early childhood education and educational technology. You can find very informative audio and video podcasts on iTunes. These podcasts can even be listened to or viewed on any PC or Mac computer without an iPod, iPad, or iPhone. You will also find amazing, instructive early childhood Internet radio stations on many of the early childhood association websites, including the National Association for the Education of Young Children (NAEYC), National Head Start Association (NHSA), National Association of Child Care Resource and Referral Agencies (NACCRRA), and others. Or you can find early childhood Internet radio on BAM! Radio Network. Many organizations and companies offer free or low-cost webinars on early childhood education that can be used to meet state licensing requirements. Just search for *early childhood webinars*. Of course, another technology-specific resource is the NAEYC Technology and Early Childhood Interest Forum website (www.techandyoungchildren.org), an excellent—and free—resource that is ideal for those who are passionate about early childhood technology.

Don't forget that the networking strategies you learn will also help you connect with parents and will help you connect parents to one another and to other resources. You will find that all of the technology skills and concepts you learn will be transferable and will have a positive impact on many areas of your life.

Basically, the takeaway is once you know a little about technology, the more you can learn about technology that can be applied in your classroom. Become a technology learner and you will become a technology leader. *Take a Giant Step*, the report from the Joan Ganz Cooney Center at Sesame Workshop, provides a glimpse of the future: "By integrating emerging digital technologies into education and lifelong learning for all professionals, beginning with teachers of children aged 3 through 8, we can establish a cost-effective and productive pathway for learning in the 21st century."

Take a Giant Step, the report from the Joan Ganz Cooney Center at Sesame Workshop, provides a glimpse of the future: "By integrating emerging digital technologies into education and lifelong learning for all professionals, beginning with teachers of children aged 3 through 8, we can establish a cost-effective and productive pathway for learning in the 21st century."

Building and Supporting Commonsense, Technology-Rich Programs

15

As an administrator, you often have to find innovative approaches to support staff members in their efforts to offer responsive and developmentally appropriate care, connect with parents, work with their peers, and implement new curricula or approaches. Many of these efforts require that you help teachers change, grow, and learn. Now, you may find yourself looking for ideas about how to evaluate, implement, and manage technology in your program. Because you are reading this chapter, we are going to assume you want to evaluate, establish, or improve a technology program in your classrooms. If you are not sure that technology makes sense for your program, read the Introduction and Chapters 1 through 3 of this book to help you create and implement a developmentally appropriate and marketable technology plan for your program. Chapters 4 through 10 provide guidance for choosing and using specific forms of technology. Although this chapter is for administrators who are ready to support their staff members in implementing classroom technology, the information is useful for anyone evaluating and considering the use of technology.

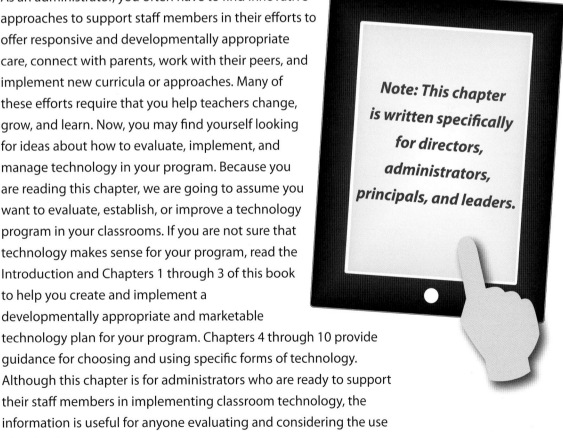

Note: This chapter is written specifically for directors, administrators, principals, and leaders.

For early childhood administrators, establishing new initiatives or sustaining an established program is part art and part science. The basics begin with the right environment. The following elements you need to set your program up for success:

- Developing a clear vision: An idea of what you want your staff to do and provide
- Knowing what is possible
- Arranging professional development for you and your staff
- Setting up an internal network of support for you and for your staff
- Setting up an external network of support for your staff
- Creating a technology plan that includes, among other things, policies and procedures
- Outlining your expectations for success
- Planning to manage resistance
- Being willing and able to communicate with parents about the technology program
- Obtaining funding
- Setting up an evaluation and reporting system

It All Starts with You!

As with curriculum implementation and other initiatives in your program, technology implementation requires a clear vision and a road map for achieving your vision. Before you set out on a road trip across the country, you must know your destination before you consult a map, right? The same can be said for embarking on any journey, and adding or enhancing your technology program is like a journey. You need to know where you want to end up so you can figure out how to get there.

Depending on your level of comfort and understanding of technology, you may also need some professional development so you can develop the big picture of what your program and your staff will need to offer commonsense, technology-rich experiences. It can be compared to looking at the entire map to determine the best route. You probably need to know all of the things you will need for your journey as well. Start by simply scanning the Suggestions for Well-Equipped Digital Centers and Classrooms form on page 178, and the Technology Self-Assessment on page 182. These tools will help you evaluate the breadth of what you will need and the types of skills your teams will need. You do not need to buy every piece of equipment or software application nor be at the "expert" level on every technology tool, but information you have as a result of filling out these two forms will give you an idea of the considerations you need to make when rounding out the overall offerings in your program.

You may not be a technology expert, but you should have a good idea of the types of technology that are available and could be useful for your classrooms. Once you gather some basic information, you will need to develop a technology plan (which is covered in depth in the next chapter). The journal for early childhood administrators, *Child Care Information Exchange*, publishes yearly reviews of the latest trends and developments in early childhood classroom technology. Reviewing those articles; checking out other online resources; consulting your social and professional networks; and talking with parents, board members, and others who may be more knowledgeable about technology will provide you with an overview of what is possible.

Evaluating your needs, making a plan (which is described in detail in Chapter 16, buying equipment and software, and putting it in the classroom are the first steps. As with everything else that is new, interesting, and innovative in your program, it is up to you to build the momentum and keep it going by using your leadership skills and doing whatever it takes to make the innovation a success. Regardless of where you are on your journey to a technology-rich program, make sure the basics are in place.

The most important thing you can do to set up your program for success with technology (and everything else you do) is to be a positive role model. You may not be a technology expert, but you need to model openness to new ideas, a willingness to try new strategies and techniques, and a collaborative spirit. Make the environment safe to try new things and fail, and turn failures into opportunities. Modeling open communication and a supportive attitude will ensure the culture in your program is safe for technology (and other) exploration.

The Vision: Knowing What Good Practice Looks Like

If you set out on a journey on a foggy day, you may miss some important road signs along the way. Similarly, you need to have a clear vision of where you are going (your technology plan) not only by knowing what you need to buy and what your staff should do, but also by knowing what teaching and learning look like in developmentally appropriate classrooms. Here are a few signposts:

Activity, noise, mess, joy, and engagement: Developmentally appropriate classrooms with or without technology are busy places. They are not chaotic, but they hum. You know it when you hear it—the steady hum of a classroom where children are engaging with one another, with the adults, and with the materials in the classroom. You should see children in learning centers using traditional materials alongside technology equipment. They should be using technology purposely and with their peers, not staring at screens by themselves for long stretches of time. The technology tools should be located throughout the room, not only over in a corner in one station or lab (although one or more stationary desktops might also be included).

Open-ended, process-oriented products of the children's activities: Developmentally appropriate classrooms often display the children's work at their eye level and for the adults to see as well. We expect the displays to vary from child to child and to show their creativity and self-expression. The same goes for products of children's work with technology tools. Look for imperfection, creativity, and individuality, not standardized pieces.

Teachers engaging with children in small groups, individually, and with the group as a whole: Teachers should work with children using technology tools. We know teachers can facilitate and extend learning when they engage with children, even during free play or choice time. The same should be true if they are using technology tools or other materials. (Of course, we are not advocating always interrupting play.) Asking open-ended and divergent questions can help children go further with their explorations, ask deeper questions, and test their hypotheses with technology, one of the many materials and tools in their classrooms.

Children should have a balance of activities in which they engage in technology exploration alone, in small groups, and with the whole class. Teachers should be involved in some of those activities, and not others, but a teacher should check in often with independent activities. Design your technology plan so teachers do not use technology:

- To "entertain" some groups of children while one teacher is working with another group,
- As a reward, or
- Without specific objectives in mind.

Balance: Technology should not be a part of every experience or project. Some experiences can be conducted more effectively with traditional materials, and some with technology tools. Teachers in commonsense, technology-rich classrooms use technology tools as another choice or option. There's no need to over-focus on balance because balance will come naturally when children select the right tool for the right job. If children are spending too much time in technology activities, the imbalance will be obvious. The hum and flow of the classroom will be disrupted.

Even in emergent programs, teachers have plans, roadmaps. However your program plans for experiences with children, you should see the balance between technology-related activities and those activities and projects that do not use technology. If you have standardized planning forms, they should clearly show that teachers are planning with balance.

There should also be balance in the types of technology tools being selected and the types of technology-related experiences being offered. The children should not always use commercially available software or websites designed specifically for children, or always select any one device or tool to the exclusion of others.

An appropriate level of challenge without excessive frustration or boredom: If teachers are using technology correctly, the children will be as engaged, excited, and motivated as they are with just about everything appropriate for their age and interests. If the experiences or tools are inappropriate for their age or their interests, you will know. The children will be frustrated or bored, and that hum for which you listen will be disrupted. You will hear whining or crying, and see children acting out. You will know it when you see it!

The needs of children who speak different languages, and those with disabilities and special needs, being met: As with everything in an accommodating classroom, you will see adaptations to meet the needs of children who are developing atypically and of those who speak other languages. There will be adaptive devices, furniture, and software.

Parent involvement and engagement being valued and evident: You should expect to see a classroom in which parents are not only welcome to engage, but they are also invited and honored. Obviously, parents are not always able to come into the program during the day, so teachers should plan ways to use technology, such as the internet, as a tool to engage and communicate with parents who cannot come into the classroom. Using overnight "backpack" exchanges with tablet computers and MP3 players is another way teachers can engage parents with technology and perhaps do their part to narrow the digital divide for families who would otherwise not have access to technology. You should see teachers planning to level the playing field for parents who speak other languages or who have children with special needs by incorporating technology tools that meet their specific needs.

> In a high-functioning, technology-rich classroom, you should not notice any difference between what you expect to see in any developmentally appropriate classroom. Only the choices of materials will be different. The classroom layout should be same, with a few well-integrated technology additions.

In general, technology makes it possible to involve parents in ways that were never possible before. Look for evidence that teachers are taking advantage of the capacity at their fingertips to make their classrooms parent friendly.

A final word on what good practice looks like, a key big-picture signpost for you as the administrator: In a high-functioning, technology-rich classroom, you should not notice any difference between what you expect to see in any developmentally appropriate classroom. Only the choices of materials will be different. The classroom layout should be same, with a few well-integrated technology additions.

What Does Your Program Need?

As you read through the Suggestions for Well-Equipped Digital Centers and Classrooms, beginning on page 178 of the Appendix, you will see the suggestions are broken down by categories: Getting Started, Good, and Advanced. Even if your goal is the "Getting Started" level, obtaining everything may be challenging. Don't give up! Break up your objectives into phases. If you were taking a cross-country road trip, you would have to stop for layovers! The same goes for your technology journey. Just start somewhere and build up slowly. Obtain whatever tools and skills are manageable for your program. Use common sense to develop a technology plan that is achievable. Set your program up for success with achievable goals.

How will you know if your program is ready to begin and take on basic technology challenges? Here is a very practical checklist you can use to see if the foundation is in place.

Basic Program Technology-Readiness Self-Assessment

Assessment Criteria	Not yet	Emerging	Complete	Steps to solve the problem or build on the strength
The senior administrator and/or leadership team support the use of technology in classrooms.				
The senior administrator and/or leadership team are able to allocate staff/volunteer resources to support the use of technology in the classrooms.				
The senior administrator and/or leadership team are able to provide funding and time for technology training for teachers and/or staff.				
Many staff members use technology for personal use and understand the basics.				
There is at least one technology "champion" on staff.				
Your program has high-speed Internet access.				
Your program has the funds to provide the basic technology needs described in the Well-Equipped Classroom List.				
You have funding to get the equipment and training needed to begin and sustain your technology efforts.				
You know where to locate grants and have the ability to apply for them.				
Your program has a technology policy.				
Your organization has measurable objectives for your technology program.				
You have sound answers about why technology use makes sense for your organization.				

Professional Development, Coaching, and Mentoring

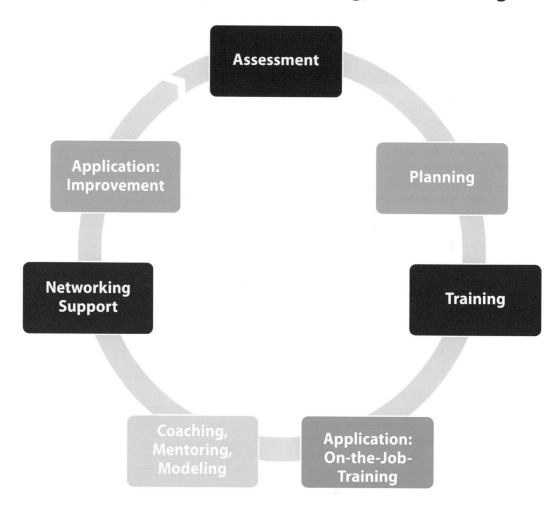

Of all of the "stuff" you need, the least tangible but most important of all will be professional development. In an ideal world, professional development includes the following:

- **Assessment:** Before you can plan professional development, you need to know what your staff members already know and what they need to know. Building a composite picture of the self-assessment on page 182, completed by all of the teachers, will help you build a plan for the entire center. The needs indicated in the self-assessments will also help you plan with individual teachers in their annual or semi-annual performance evaluations.
- **Planning:** Once you have a baseline for what your staff needs to know, it's time to plan. Include internal champions in your planning team.
- **Training:** You will need to determine which type(s) of formal training will work best for your staff members.

- **Application: On-the-Job Training:** When staff members have completed formal training (if needed), it's time for them to practice and apply what they have learned. There is nothing like on-the-job training and opportunities to practice the skills learned.

- **Coaching, Mentoring, and Modeling:** As teachers begin to apply what they have learned in the classroom, they are likely to need support, encouragement, and guidance. The teachers will turn to you, their peers, and your program's internal technology champions for technical support, advice, and encouragement. Even if you do not consider yourself experienced in technology, the teachers will look to you for cues about how to handle the disruption caused by innovation and how to network for support. Do not underestimate how much they look to you for subtle indications of how they should handle their response to technology integration.

- **Networking Support:** Teachers will need encouragement and time to connect with internal and external networks of support. You and the technology champions may need to offer ideas and links to online and/or real-life networks where teachers can get more information, support, and new ideas.

- **Application: Improvement:** The professional development process is a continual cycle in which teachers learn, apply, reassess, and apply again to make incremental improvements to their programs. This cycle is probably even more apparent and important to the process of technology integration. The process for some may be slower and more incremental than others, but it is a cycle nonetheless.

Technology Professional Development Champions

A good professional development program starts with a strong, diverse team of supportive and engaged people who can provide a broad set of perspectives. Gather a team of representatives from your staff, board, and other consultants who will provide guidance throughout the professional development planning process. You want to choose people who are as determined as you to help the program grow a sound technology program.

Professional Development Assessment and Planning

You and your technology professional development team need to take a look at the big picture first. To begin, you and your staff members can take the technology professional development self-assessment on page 182, or any technology assessment tool you think is relevant. Review the completed forms to get an idea of the strengths and weaknesses throughout the program. Take a look at the different types of formal training outlined in Chapter 14 to determine what combination of training makes sense in the overall scheme. Break down into phases all of the content you want to tackle. Remember, professional development is a journey, not a sprint.

Ideally, you would participate in every formal training session you plan for staff members, so they know you wouldn't expect them to do anything you would not do yourself. Even if you are already an expert in the topic of the training, you can play a role as a leader in the session.

Learning theory tells us that one-shot formal training sessions only go so far, especially if they are not followed by opportunities to apply what has been learned and to reflect on the outcome of the application. This is especially true of technology. If learners do not apply what they have learned in real-life experiences soon after the training and do not repeat these experiences, it is easy for learners to forget the skills.

Once your staff has participated in any of the types of formal training listed in Chapter 14, offer your teachers opportunities for them to apply what has been learned. Hopefully the training will inspire the teachers to implement what they have learned in the classroom right away. If the training was good, chances are that their motivation will be high, and they will be raring to get started with the children.

This is also the best time for you to ask questions about the training and to encourage the teachers to use what they have learned. If they don't feel ready to implement their skills and knowledge with the children, provide time for teachers to practice what they have learned, and offer to connect them with someone who can coach them. This would also be a great time to show your staff members some of the external supports available to them through social networking sites, forums, email discussion groups, and community professional learning networks.

If you have learned enough about the tools and skills, this is when modeling would be a good idea. While you probably won't have time to be a personal coach or mentor to every staff member, you can be a good role model by applying what you know or have learned in settings where the staff can make the most of the experience—right in their classrooms. You probably already spend a lot of time observing and interacting in every classroom in your center. When you make your rounds, join in the fun, using the technology alongside the children and the teachers. Demonstrate your willingness to roll up your sleeves and join in.

Evaluating Commercially Available Software Designed Specifically for Children

You may want to include your technology professional development team in making decisions about appropriate software. You may want to assemble a new team composed of staff members who have demonstrated success with technology in their classrooms, or who are highly motivated about your technology program efforts. Be sure to include a few parents who support and champion your technology efforts. This is a great way to educate them about developmentally appropriate practice and software evaluation resources, as well as to engage them in authentically necessary activities.

In the Appendix, we provide an evaluation tool called The Commonsense Approach to Developmentally Appropriate Evaluation of Software, Websites, and Apps Developed for Young Children. The form was derived from existing evaluation tools by Susan Haugland (Haugland & Wright, 1997) and Warren Buckleitner (Buckleitner, 1985). These are great resources to use to make decisions about which software and apps are good matches for your program objectives. Of course, you may find other great resources online, but be careful to use only those that were developed by reputable, independent sources that will not benefit from your purchases. In other words, manufacturers are great sources of information about their products' features and benefits, but they are not an independently reliable source of information about how good or appropriate the product will be for your setting. Also look for resources that offer advice specifically for early childhood education, not older children, and not products designed for entertainment.

You will find a wealth of ideas about using other types of technology tools in the chart titled A Few Ideas about How to Use Software, Apps, and Online Systems Developed for Use by Adults for Open-Ended Projects and Experiences on page 63. This list includes tools that are not designed for children but are essential for a well-rounded program. In fact, your classrooms could offer robust technology experiences using these applications without using a lot of commercially developed children's applications. This could be one way to begin your program without overspending on purchased titles. It is certainly worth exploring.

Regardless of what you use to evaluate the tools for your technology program, the evaluation should be systematic and include more than two people. You may also want to refer to online reviews published by experts and by other users. We have listed several resources for software reviews in our Resources section on page 175.

Technology Plans for Commonsense, Technology-Rich Programs

16

As you prepare to evaluate and integrate technology in your center or school, you've identified your goals so you can figure out how to get from where you are (point A) to where you want to be (point B). You have considered your need to stop along the way, but you probably want specific directions you can consult throughout the journey. That would be your program's technology plan.

Your technology planning process should do the following:

- **Be collaborative and inclusive.** You will want to include teachers, parents, board members, community members, and anyone who can offer some advice about technology, funding, and accounting. But keep the group small enough to handle. We recommend including no more than eight people.
- **Be compressed.** This is not a process that should take years. In fact, it needs to correlate to your budget-planning process, so it should not even take months. Make it your goal to complete the process and have a written plan in a month to six weeks.
- **Result in a plan that can actually be implemented.** It should not be so ambitious that it is impossible. Consider developing a plan that is broken into phases that can be accomplished over five years.
- **Be based on realistic financing and funding.**

The resulting technology plan should cover these elements:

- **Assessment of technology readiness**—The prerequisite building blocks that need to be in place
- **Policies**—A set of rules and procedures that guide the safe and appropriate operation of technology in your program
- **Objectives**—The expectations you have for measurable success

- **Professional development**—How you will keep staff members informed and trained
- **Tech support**—The people who will manage technical solutions to problems with devices and software
- **Tech resource team**—The people to whom staff members can turn with questions and problems related to implementation
- **Resources**—Material and human resource allocation
- **Funding and budgeting**—Plans to find and allocate funding for all of aspects of the plan
- **Implementation**—How to roll out, evaluate, revise, and sustain your plan
- **Evaluation**—Tools and resources to determine if the objectives have been met

Developing a technology plan should not be done in isolation. You must form a working group or committee of people who will join you to develop the technology plan. Technology plans don't have to be huge documents, but they do need to address all these critical elements. Most of the elements of the technology plan are addressed throughout this book.

It is essential that your program develop responsive and responsible technology policies that address, among other things:

- Managing technology access
- Protecting privacy and confidentiality, and preventing exploitation
- Facing and managing challenges presented by social networking and other emerging technology tools and systems
- Avoiding inappropriate use
- Providing guidelines for acceptable use
- Creating procedures for suggesting and evaluating new tools
- Including parents
- Meeting the needs of children who are developing atypically and of those who speak other languages
- Ensuring bias-free and violence-free experiences for children
- Supporting digital literacy

There are many resources to help you design a program technology policy. The NAEYC technology position statement, *Technology and Interactive Media as Tools in Early Childhood Programs Serving Children from Birth through Age 8, is* the guiding document. But you will probably need more guidance along the way. There are many books on the market, but few are specific to early childhood educational settings. *Clicking Smarter: School Technology Policies that Work!,* written by Christopher Wells for secondary schools as a joint publication of the American Association of School Administrators and the National Association of Secondary School Principals, is clearly written and well conceived. You may want to add this book as a resource to guide your policy development efforts, but you will likely need to modify what you learn for your early childhood setting.

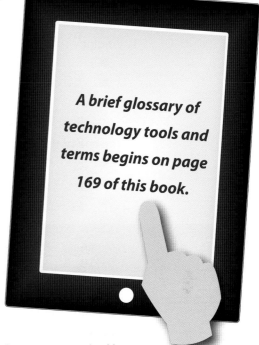

A brief glossary of technology tools and terms begins on page 169 of this book.

If you struggle to plan for your infrastructure, look for help throughout your organization—the board members, parents, other staff members, staff member's families, and even the local business community. You may want to connect with other early childhood programs in your community that have introduced technology, to learn from their experiences. Colleges and universities may have access to support for programs implementing technology integration.

Helping Teachers Plan for Technology Integration

Rolling out your technology plan should be incremental. One critical factor in your successes will be helping teachers plan for their roles in the process. As with everything else you do, helping teachers organize themselves to meet challenges requires that you provide them with tools. The following form, Yearly Classroom Technology Plan for Teachers, is a tool you can provide to teachers to use as is, or you can modify the form based on your program's needs.

Yearly Classroom Technology Plan for Teachers

By the end of the school year, children in my class should be able to (as it relates to technology):

-
-
-

By the end of the school year, children in my class should know (as it relates to technology):

-
-
-

	The technology-related content and developmental objectives:
Math	
Science	
Social Studies	
Language and Literacy	
Physical Development	
Social	
Emotional	
Approaches to Learning	

	I will integrate technology into each interest area in my classroom by adding:
Dramatic Play	
Art	
Sand/Water	
Library	
Blocks	
Circle	
Manipulatives/Games	

	I will integrate technology into each interest area in my classroom by adding (continued):
Science	
Cooking	
Outdoors	
Writing	
Math	
Other	

I will ensure equal access to technology for all children in my classroom, including those with special needs and those whose primary language is not English by:

-
-
-

I will engage and involve parents in my classroom and ensure equal access to technology for all families in my program by:

-
-
-

My technology-related professional development goals are to:

-
-
-

I will share my technology-related skills and knowledge with others by:

-
-
-

Conclusion

Being an early childhood educator is challenging, rewarding, and often exciting. It can also be especially complex in our technology-driven world. You may feel exhilarated by the opportunities technology tools present for your classroom, or you may feel overwhelmed. You may feel both! Regardless of your emotions, this is an extraordinary time to be an early childhood educator.

Whether you are experienced with technology integration or new to it, approach the challenges and opportunities presented by technology with an open mind, a willingness to experiment, and an interest in discovering what works best for the children in your program. Teachers and administrators who are experienced in technology need to take a leadership role. Share your knowledge and skills, and make it safe for staff members who are fearful, resistant, or just new to the process by being generous and patient.

If you are new to technology integration, take the process one step at a time. Evaluate what is possible, consider the developmental needs and abilities of the children in your classroom, and add a tool or technique that you understand and that meets the needs of the children. Focus on the tools that you think will have the greatest impact. Listen to your heart and your good intuition to make choices. Apply your common sense to the process, and partner with a more experienced coach or mentor.

Interactivity is the heart of good early childhood practice with or without the addition of technology tools. Plan carefully. Evaluate tools and processes, and add tools that engage children, offer appropriate challenges, and limit frustration. Focus on planning for *interactive* experiences as you add technology to your program.

We hope that, no matter where you are on the continuum of technology adoption and implementation, this book has offered a commonsense lens through which you can understand the debate, evaluate technology tools, and decide what works best for the children in your classroom as you journey through technology in early childhood settings.

Glossary

Hardware: Hardware means the physical elements or equipment used to enable people to interact with software programs or otherwise perform digital tasks. Hardware includes:

- **Desktop computers:** Desktop computers are stationed on a desk or other flat surface. They can include a central processing unit (CPU), a keyboard, monitor, and mouse. They are less expensive than laptops and offer stability that can be useful for placement in the writing or library centers or other areas where you are likely to want children and teachers to interact with computers. Desktop computers can be more durable and less prone to theft due to their size. They also offer some measure of adaptability for children with certain special physical needs.

- **Mobile computing: Laptops, mobile multi-touch devices such as tablets and iPads:** While mobile technology can be more expensive, the price range can vary depending on the primary use of the device. Overall, laptops and desktops are designed to perform thousands of discrete tasks depending on the software that is installed, but smartphones and tablet computers offer less functionality and are often more appropriate for what is commonly referred to as "light" computing. For completely integrated, highly interactive, and engaging use in early childhood settings, tablets offer extraordinary functionality and incredible promise. There are literally millions of affordable applications (or "apps") that can be downloaded to tablets and smartphones in an instant.

  If your budget is healthy, selecting the appropriate types of computers should not be an either/or proposition. In an ideal world, you would place a traditional computer (laptop or desktop) in certain areas of the room, and have a tablet or two that could be used anywhere in the room on field trips, on the playground, in the kitchen, or in the office. You might even pop it in classroom backpacks to share with families.

  Smartphones are "ultra mobile" devices that have proven to be essential for communication by phone and/or text messaging and computing on the go. They are the perfect companion for emergencies and "gotta have it now" information. While the smaller screen size limits the functionality for viewing, the flexibility of smartphones is unbeatable because they can fit into your pocket and are available in an instant.

- **Peripherals: Printers, camera, mice, touch screens, furniture, and adaptive devices:** The term *peripherals* means the devices that are attached to your computer with cables, Bluetooth devices, or wireless networks. More often than not in our mobile computing environment, computers and devices are connected through wireless connections that are operated through hubs. You can connect multiple computers to one another, the Internet, and to printers and other devices. You can even connect mice, keyboards, and monitors to your computer wirelessly.

  When you develop your computer plan, consider how you will connect your devices, and plan the space around your requirements. Think about what types of equipment you will need to meet the needs of the children in your program and how that will fuse into your classroom.

  If you will have desktops, think about ergonomics and selecting the size of the surface and the chairs. You will need to consider the type of monitor, keyboard, and mice to buy. As a general rule of thumb, there's no need to spend a lot of money on specially designed, kid-friendly keyboards or mice unless you need to accommodate children with physical disabilities.

  It is a good idea to invest as much as you can afford into the monitor to get a very large touch-screen model, unless you have an interactive whiteboard or interactive multi-touch table. Touch screens are monitors that allow the user to interact by touching the screen instead of interacting through the mouse or keyboard. They are much more user-friendly and intuitive than keyboards and mice when used with the right software.

- **Interactive whiteboards and multi-touch display tables:** Interactive whiteboards and multi-touch display tables, such as the Smartboard and SMART Table (brand names), are amazing tools that can replace chalkboards and whiteboards. It is possible for large groups to interact with interactive whiteboards. Much like touch screens, children and teachers can use their fingers to interact with the images on interactive displays.

  Typically, you will need a computer (desktop or laptop) to project the applications onto the multi-touch device. Interactive whiteboards are wall hung, but multi-touch tables are like a hybrid of a light table and a computer. The interactivity is similar to the experience of using a tablet computer but on a larger scale that allows groups of children to work together. While these very cool multi-touch devices have a lot of potential for creative and divergent activities, they are currently very expensive. They are not affordable for every classroom but would make fantastic additions given a healthy technology budget.

Software: Desktop, Internet-delivered, and apps: Software means the technology you can't really touch. Software is the instructions computers need to work.

- **Operating systems:** One type of software every computer needs, no matter what type of computer, is an operating system. Personal computers (PCs) and devices not developed by Apple run on Windows or Linux operating systems. Mac computers, iPads, iPods, and iPhones use Apple operating systems. Your device will come with the operating system already installed. Operating systems tell the computer how to work with the user, other devices, and the other various software applications on the machine to complete tasks or display images.

- **Desktop software:** Desktop software means the software is installed on the computer and "lives" on the hard drive. Every time the user accesses the software, the computer looks on the hard drive for the instructions it needs to do the task. Software that is purchased from a store is provided to the user on CD or DVD or other storage media, or it is downloaded from the Internet. The user must install the application by inserting the storage medium into the computer or downloading software and installing it. Boxed software is becoming less common. Developers are delivering desktop software via the Internet and cloud computing or software as a service (SaaS) computing.

- **Desktop software versus cloud computing software:** Software delivered by the cloud are applications that are stored on the manufacturer's or service provider's computers. The user typically licenses the use of the software by subscribing for a specific period of time, and every time the application is used, it is being accessed through the provider's computers. For example, Yahoo, Google, and Facebook are all application service providers. They all offer free options, but they provide software for users and store the data on their computers. There are hundreds of thousands of software applications available for subscription or one-time fees as well. For example, you may use ProCare, EZCare, or ChildPlus in your center. These companies offer cloud computing (and desktop software) applications. Over the coming years, cloud computing will replace desktop software.

- **Apps:** You may have wondered what an app is. Apps are application software, or smaller pieces of software typically designed to do discrete tasks. They are less robust than complete software applications, but they can be very powerful in their interactivity. Most of the references you hear today refer to mobile apps, or apps that are installed on smartphones or other mobile devices such as tablet computers. Apps are very powerful because they are often less expensive than a complete software bundle, are highly focused and interactive, and are available on demand.

If you have a smartphone or other mobile device, you are walking around with software stores in your pocket! You can buy and download complete bundled software packages and apps or use cloud computing whenever or wherever there is a connection to the Internet. Now that's flexibility!

Low-tech tools: CD players, MP3 players, digital cameras, webcams, microphones, listening stations, video cameras, and other devices and appliances: Some of the common appliances used in classrooms can really be classified as technology. Every time you play music, take a photo, or use a microwave in your classroom, you are using technology. We classify those devices as low-tech tools, but they are very important in a connected classroom. You will need to consider how to extend your current use of low-tech tools to fit into your technology plan alongside the more cutting-edge tools.

- **Digital still and video cameras:** Two of the most valuable tools you will be able to extend when used with computers and other devices are digital still and video cameras. Digital cameras have revolutionized the ability to capture classroom moments affordably and share them in an instant. With digital cameras (both video and still) you can take as many photos as you want without worrying about the cost of film and printing. Now, you don't have to print photos to share them (although you may still want to do that often). Best of all, high-quality still and video cameras are often built into cell phones and smartphones as well as mobile tablets, making them highly portable and flexible enough to share the images with people on the spot. You can now be on a field trip, record a video, and share it via email or social networking sites with a few easy clicks.

  Storing photographs and videos on digital devices not only makes them easier to share, but there are also creative ways to manipulate the files and use them in projects. Children can use photo editing software designed especially for them, or use some of the easier applications designed for adults. Making books, scrapbooks, and even movies is extremely easy with desktop software as well as Internet-driven software. There are hundreds of Internet applications like Vimeo, Flickr, Snapfish, and others designed to store, edit, and share photos and videos. Digital still and video cameras are among the most essential, affordable, and creative technology tools you can include in your technology plan.

- **Webcams:** Webcams, which are often built into many mobile computers, also allow you to stream (send over the Internet in real time) video as it happens. If you are using a desktop, there are also webcams that can plug into your computer and offer a high degree of flexibility, even though they are tethered to a stationary machine. Teamed with computer microphones, speakers, headsets, and Internet service, webcams allow you to talk directly with people anywhere in the world and see their images as you speak with one another.

Face-to-face digital communication has become commonly referred to as "Skyping." (Skype was the first application to provide widely available voice over Internet protocol (VOIP) service, or video chat.) The potential for video chat with children in the classroom is enormous. Just think about taking pen pals to the next level, allowing children to talk to deployed military parents, or connecting children who speak different languages.

- **Digital music devices:** You know all of those CDs (or maybe even vinyl records) you use to play music in your classroom? Now, all of that music can be stored on MP3 players or iPods, computers, or even smartphones. It's easy to connect these devices to speakers for use in your classroom, and ditching the CDs and records simply saves valuable space. Digital music doesn't scratch, warp, or get lost. You can transfer your music onto your digital devices, or you can buy new music through online stores and download it directly to your digital devices. Older children can even select the music and play it with a click. Children can listen through headsets or speakers attached to the device. Children can also record their voices and play it back using these devices, which is a functionality that offers almost limitless opportunities for creative and divergent explorations. Despite the affordability and flexibility of digital music devices, CD players are still a viable option. There's no doubt that music and voice recording will always be an important part of preschool classrooms, so including devices for these purposes is essential.

Internet access and internal networking: This sounds complicated, right? It's not that bad. At the foundation of all the fun technology tool plans are the boring basics, which include Internet access.

- **Internet service:** Because Internet service providers (ISPs) are fairly regional, we won't provide specific advice about carriers. Typically, you will buy the service from a provider such as Verizon, Comcast, or Cox, and pay for it on a monthly basis. The prices range dramatically depending on geography and the plan you select. The number of devices you have connecting at one time and the types of computing you plan to do will determine your selection. Your ISP will help you make the right decision for your organization.

The ISP will run a line to your center and install an outlet (or several) in your center. They will connect a modem using an Ethernet cable. The modem is the device that makes the Internet available to all of the computers in the program.

- **Internal networking:** Networking means connecting the computers in your program to one another, to the printers, scanners, and other equipment, and to the Internet. Networking can be very simple or very complex, depending on your program's needs. You can set up computers that connect to one printer and the Internet, or you can connect all of your computers to each other.

Once the connection to the Internet is established, you have to decide if you want a wireless (Wi-Fi) network to connect the computers to each other and other devices, or if you want to install Ethernet cables to each machine. If you want a wireless system, you will add a wireless hub to the modem, and your computers will communicate with it across the airwaves, using the operating systems on each computer. This is what your Wi-Fi configuration will look like:

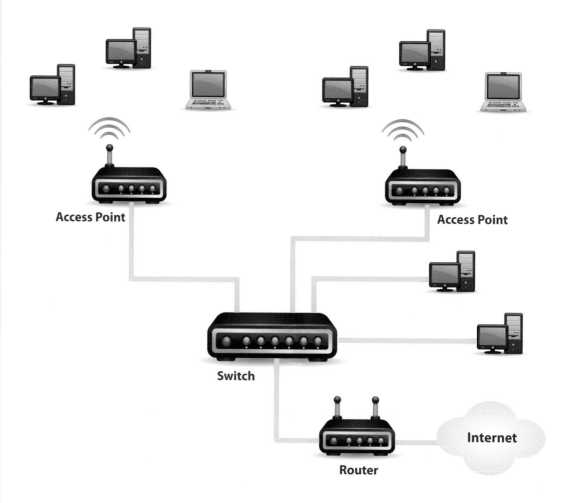

Resources

Websites to Visit for Research, Reports, and Updates

Center for Technology in Learning at SRI (http://ctl.sri.com)

Children's Technology Review (http://childrenstech.com)

Common Sense Media (www.commonsensemedia.org)

ECETech.net (www.ecetech.net)

Federal Office of Educational Technology
(www2.ed.gov/about/offices/list/os/technology/index.html)

The Fred Rogers Center for Early Learning and Children's Media (www.fredrogerscenter.org)

International Society for Technology in Education (www.iste.org)

The Joan Ganz Cooney Center at Sesame Workshop (www.joanganzcooneycenter.org)

National Association for the Education of Young Children (www.naeyc.org)

New America Foundation, Early Ed Watch Blog (http://earlyed.newamerica.net/blogmain)

PBS Kids (http://pbskids.org)

Books, Papers, Reports, and Position Statements

American Academy of Pediatrics. 2001. *Children, Adolescents, and Television*. Position statement. Available at http://aappolicy.aappublications.org/cgi/reprint/pediatrics;107/2/423.pdf.

Barron, B., Cayton-Hodges, G., Bofferding, L., Copple, C., Darling-Hammond, L., & Levine, M.H. 2001. *Take a giant step: A blueprint for teaching young children in a digital age*. Report from the Joan Ganz Cooney Center at Sesame Workshop and Stanford University. Available at http://joanganzcooneycenter.org/Reports-31.html.

Bredekamp, S. & Copple, C. 2010. *Developmentally appropriate practice in early childhood programs serving birth through age 8,* third edition. Washington, DC: NAEYC.

Clements, D. & Sarama, J. 2003a. Strip mining for gold: Research and policy in educational technology: A response to "Fool's Gold". *AACE Journal*. 11(1), 7–69.

Clements, D., & Sarama, J. 2003b. Young children and technology: What does the research say? *Young Children* 58(6): 34–40.

Common Sense Media. 2011. Zero to eight: Children's media use in America. Available at www.commonsensemedia.org/sites/default/files/research/zerotoeightfinal2011.pdf.

Gillespie, C. W. & Beisser, S. R. 2001. Developmentally appropriate LOGO computer programming with young children. *Information Technology in Childhood Education*, 232-247.

Gillespie, C. W. 2004. Seymour Papert's vision for early childhood education? A descriptive study of preschoolers and kindergarteners in discovery-based, Logo-rich classrooms. *Early Childhood Research and Practice*, 6(1). Available online at http://ecrp.uiuc.edu/v6n1/gillespie.html

Guernsey, L. 2007. *Into the minds of babes: How screen time affects children from birth to age five*. New York: Basic Books.

Haugland, S. & Wright, J. 1997. *Young children and technology: A world of discovery*. New York: Allyn and Bacon.

Haugland, S. 2005. Selecting or upgrading software and Web sites in the classroom. *Early Childhood Education Journal*. 32(5) 329-340.

Haugland, S. W. 2004. Early childhood classrooms in the 21st century: Using computers to maximize learning. In Hirschbuhl, J. *Computers in Education*, annual edition. New York: McGraw Hill.

International Reading Association. 2009. New literacies and 21st century technologies: A position statement of the International Reading Association. Brochure. Newark, DE: International Reading Association.

NAEYC & the Fred Rogers Center for Early Learning and Children's Media at Saint Vincent College. 2012. *Technology and Interactive Media as Tools in Early Childhood Programs Serving Children from Birth through Age 8*. Joint position statement. Washington, DC: NAEYC; Latrobe, PA: Fred Rogers Center for Early Learning and Children's Media at Saint Vincent College.

Matte, C. Limiting computer use time for kids, Available at http://familyinternet.about.com/od/introtofamilycomputing/a/LimitComputer.htm.

Office of Educational Technology, U.S. Department of Education. 2010. *Transforming American education: Learning powered by technology*. Available at www.ed.gov/sites/default/files/NETP-2010-final-report.pdf.

Papert, S. 1993. *Mindstorms: Children, computers, and powerful ideas*. New York: Basic Books.

Parette, H. P., Quesenberry, A. C., & Blum, C. 2010. Missing the boat with technology usage in early childhood settings: A 21st century view of developmentally appropriate practices. *Early Childhood Education Journal*, 37(5), 335-343.

Thouvenelle, S. & C. J. Bewick. 2003. *Completing the Computer Puzzle: A Guide for Early Childhood Educators*, Boston: Allyn & Bacon.

Appendix

Charts and Forms

Digital Literacy Basic Skills Self-Assessment

Suggestions for Well-Equipped Digital Centers and Classrooms

Weekly Play Chart

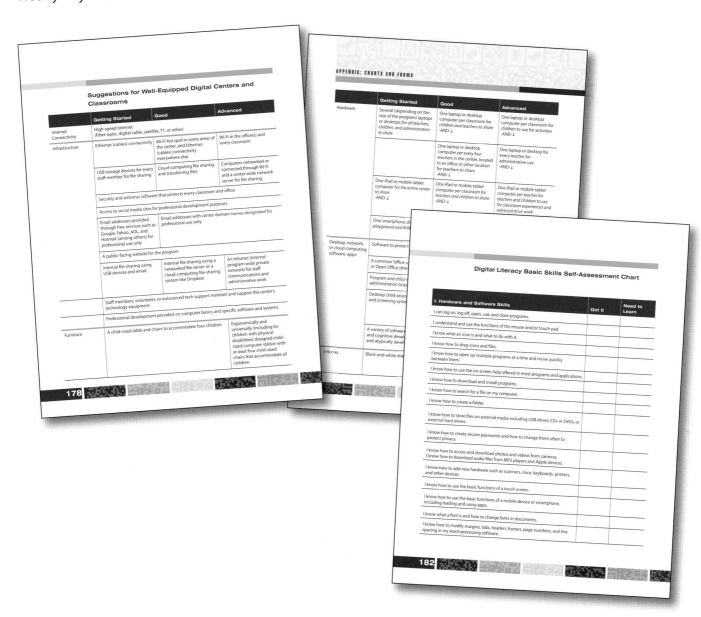

Suggestions for Well-Equipped Digital Centers and Classrooms

	Getting Started	**Good**	**Advanced**
Internet Connectivity	High-speed Internet (Fiber-optic, digital cable, satellite, T1, or other)		
Infrastructure	Ethernet (cables) connectivity	Wi-Fi hot spot in some areas of the center, and Ethernet (cables) connectivity everywhere else	Wi-Fi in the office(s) and every classroom
	USB storage devices for every staff member for file sharing	Cloud-computing file sharing and transferring files	Computers networked or connected through Wi-Fi and a center-wide network server for file sharing
	Security and antivirus software that protects every classroom and office		
	Access to social media sites for professional development purposes		
	Email addresses provided through free services such as Google, Yahoo, AOL, and Hotmail (among others) for professional use only	Email addresses with center domain names designated for professional use only	
	A public-facing website for the program		
	Internal file sharing using USB devices and email.	Internal file sharing using a networked file server or a cloud computing file-sharing system like Dropbox	An Intranet (internal program-wide private network) for staff communications and administrative work
	Staff members, volunteers, or outsourced tech support maintain and support the center's technology equipment		
	Professional development provided on computer basics and specific software and systems		
Furniture	A child-sized table and chairs to accommodate four children		Ergonomically and universally (including for children with physical disabilities) designed child-sized computer station with at least four child-sized chairs that accommodate all children

	Getting Started	Good	Advanced
Hardware	Several (depending on the size of the program) laptops or desktops for *all teachers, children, and administrators to share*	One laptop or desktop computer per classroom for *children and teachers to share* -AND-↓	One laptop or desktop computer per classroom for *children* to use for activities -AND-↓
		One laptop or desktop computer *per every four teachers* in the center, located in an office or other location for teachers to share -AND-↓	One laptop or desktop for every *teacher* for administrative use -AND-↓
	One iPad or mobile tablet computer *for the entire center to share* -AND-↓	One iPad or mobile tablet computer *per classroom for teachers and children to share* -AND-↓	One iPad or mobile tablet computer *per teacher for teachers and children to use for classroom experiences and administrative work* -AND-↓
	One smartphone *shared by all teachers in the center for playground and field trip use*		One smartphone for every teacher for emergencies and ultra-mobile computing
Desktop, network, or cloud computing software, apps	Software to protect children from accessing inappropriate sites		
	A common "office suite" of software applications, such as Microsoft Office, Google Apps, iWork, or Open Office (these applications will be used for children and teachers)		
	Program and child-management software for enrollment, payment, and other program administration tasks		
	Desktop child-assessment and screening systems	Child-assessment and screening systems that are "networked" or share information throughout the center	Internet-based, cloud computing child-assessment and screening systems
	A variety of software applications for children to meet social, emotional, physical, language, and cognitive development objectives at each age that align with the standards for typically and atypically developing children in your program and your state		
E-Books	Black-and-white electronic readers for children and teachers		Color electronic readers or tablet computers for children and teachers

	Getting Started	Good	Advanced
Peripherals	One networked or cabled networked printer for all classrooms and administrators to share or One printer for all classrooms and administrators to share using USB mass-media storage devices to transfer files or a cloud computing file storage system	One networked or cabled networked printer for all classrooms to share and at least one networked printer for all administrators to share	One wireless or cabled networked printer for each classroom and at least one networked printer for all administrators to share
		One local (stand-alone) printer connected by a cable to a stationary computer per classroom for children -AND-↓	One networked printer for children -AND-↓
		One local (stand-alone) printer connected by a cable to a stationary computer for all teachers to share -AND-↓	One networked printer for teachers -AND-↓
		One local (stand-alone) printer connected by a cable for administrators	One networked printer for administrators
	One digital still camera for the center	One digital still camera for each classroom	One digital still camera for each teacher
	One digital video camera for the center to share		One digital video camera for each classroom
	One USB microphone and four USB headsets or four USB microphone/headset combinations		
	High-quality speakers that can be used with a desktop, laptop, tablet, or MP3 player		
	One internal or external webcam		
			One interactive multi-touch table with appropriate devices/software to operate

	Getting Started	Good	Advanced
Talking pens/ Smartpens			Five Smartpens with programmable stickers for teacher-created content that can be used in small groups or choice time
Digital voice recorders	One digital voice recorder for the program	One digital voice recorder for each classroom	One digital voice recorder for each teacher/ assistant/specialist
Reading machines			One card reader or reading machine per classroom
Overhead projectors	One overhead or LCD projector for the program	One overhead or LCD projector for every five classrooms	One overhead or LCD projector for every classroom
MP3 music players/iPods with headset	One MP3 music player or iPod with headset for each classroom	Five MP3 music players or iPods with headsets per classroom	One MP3 music player or iPod with headset for each child

Digital Literacy Basic Skills Self-Assessment

I. Hardware and Software Skills	Got It	Need to Learn
I can log on, log off, open, use, and close programs.		
I understand and use the functions of the mouse and/or touch pad.		
I know what an icon is and what to do with it.		
I know how to drag icons and files.		
I know how to open up multiple programs at a time and move quickly between them.		
I know how to use the on-screen help offered in most programs and applications.		
I know how to download and install programs.		
I know how to search for a file on my computer.		
I know how to create a folder.		
I know how to store files on external media including USB drives, CDs or DVDs, or external hard drives.		
I know how to create secure passwords and how to change them often to protect privacy.		
I know how to access and download photos and videos from cameras. I know how to download audio files from MP3 players and Apple devices.		
I know how to add new hardware such as scanners, mice, keyboards, printers, and other devices.		
I know how to use the basic functions of a touch screen.		
I know how to use the basic functions of a mobile device or smartphone, including loading and using apps.		
I know what a font is and how to change fonts in documents.		
I know how to modify margins, tabs, headers, footers, page numbers, and line spacing in my word-processing software.		

I. Hardware and Software Skills (continued)	Got It	Need to Learn
I know how to edit, copy, cut, and paste a block of text in my word-processing software.		
I know how to create a table in a word-processing document or presentation.		
I can use the spell-checker tool in my word-processing software.		
I know how to insert graphics and other files into a document or presentation.		
I know how to save a document, presentation, or spreadsheet and use Save As to change the format or saved location of the document.		
I know how to create a simple spreadsheet with rows, columns, and headings in spreadsheet software.		
I know how to create a simple presentation using presentation software, complete with photos and other graphics.		

II. Internet Skills	Got It	Need to Learn
I know how to connect to the Internet.		
I know how to go directly to a website using the site URL address.		
I know how to search for a website using a search engine such as Google or Yahoo.		
I know how to save, print, or forward a webpage.		
I know how to bookmark webpages so I can go back to them later.		
I know how to download, decompress, and open documents and programs (for example, applications, presentation files, PDF files).		
I know how to log on and log off of password-protected websites.		
I know how to construct a search for an exact phrase.		

III. Online Safety, Security, and Privacy	Got It	Need to Learn
I know how to use and maintain up-to-date antivirus and security software programs, and I use them regularly.		
I know at least three ways to avoid having my computer become infected with a virus.		
I know how to manage my computer password and the passwords for the various systems I need to use.		
I know how to avoid email and online scams.		
I never share my password, username, Social Security number, credit card, banking information, or other sensitive information online unless I am confident the site is secure.		
I know what *https://* means before the www in a website URL.		
I know how to adjust my security settings on social media sites.		

IV. Media Literacy: Communication and Locating and Using Credible Information Online	Got It	Need to Learn
I have a personal email address and know how to use it.		
I have a work-related email address and know how to use it.		
I know what a listserv or electronic discussion group is.		
I know how to attend a webinar.		
I know how to manage and attend online classes.		
I know how to participate in online chats.		
I use social media sites like Facebook, LinkedIn, and Twitter, and I know how to stay safe on these sites.		
I understand the difference between blogs and websites.		
I know how to find credible information on the Internet.		
I know how to evaluate the credibility of a website or the information on the website based on the authority of the website owner, its accuracy, and objectivity.		

IV. Media Literacy: Communication and Locating and Using Credible Information Online (continued)	Got It	Need to Learn
I know that all images, words, and sounds, except information explicitly said to be "in the public domain" or tagged with a Creative Commons registration mark, may be copyrighted, and use of these original expressions may require permission of the copyright holder.		
I know how to determine the source of a website.		
I know how to critically evaluate the information I read online based on the source.		

V. Online Consumer Awareness	Got It	Need to Learn
I can discern between paid advertisements and other information on websites, social networks, and search engines.		
I understand that when I fill out forms online, I may be "opting in" to receive email from companies.		
I know how to avoid in-app purchases I do not intend to make.		
I know how to determine if a website is safe and secure for online purchases.		
I know how to locate contact information for the companies with which I do business online.		

Weekly Play Chart

Child's Name_____ Date_____

	Monday	Tuesday	Wednesday	Thursday	Friday
Art					
Blocks					
Cooking Play					
Dramatic Play					
Library					
Manipulatives					
Math Center					
Outdoors					
Water/ Sand					
Writing Center					

Index